Walks Around Edingthorpe

By Gill Cullingford

Published by G Cullingford
© Copyright Gill Cullingford 2021

Walks Around Edingthorpe

All rights reserved.

The right of Gill Cullingford to be identified as the author of this work has been asserted in accordance with the Copyright, Designs and Patents Act 1988.
No part of this publication may be reproduced, stored in a retrieval system or transmitted in any form or by any means, electronic, mechanical, photocopying, recording or otherwise, nor translated into machine language without the written permission of the publisher.

Conditions of sale

This book is sold subject to the condition that it shall not, by way of trade or otherwise, be lent, re-sold, hired out or otherwise circulated in any form of binding or cover other than that in which it is published and without a similar condition including this condition being imposed on the subsequent purchaser.

ISBN: 9798708988850

Cover photograph: Edingthorpe Crossroads © Gill Cullingford

Contents   Page

Introduction   4

The Paston Way   7

From Edingthorpe Church:

Walk 1: Edingthorpe circular (2.3 miles)   8
Walk 2: The Three Churches (4.5 miles)   16
Walk 3: Edingthorpe to the Sea (1.5 or 4 miles) 25
Walk 4: A Walk around Witton (4.9 miles)   30

From Edingthorpe Green:

Walk 5: The Green to Edingthorpe Church (3.2 miles)   36
Walk 6: Historic transport: the old branch line and
         the canal (3.5 miles)   40
Walk 7: The Green to the Knapton Angels (3.2 miles)   47
Walk 8: The Butterfly Walk (0.9 or 2.7 miles)   52
Walk 9: Pigneys Wood (1.0 or 3.5 miles)   58

From Royston Bridge:

Walk 10: Royston Bridge to Ebridge Mill (3.5 miles)   64
Walk 11: Around Little London (2.5 miles)   70

From Bacton Wood:

Walk 12: Bacton Wood circular (1.3 miles)   74

Acknowledgements   79

Walks Around Edingthorpe

Edingthorpe is a small village near North Walsham in North Norfolk, set in lovely countryside. It is thought to date back to the 11C, its name originating from 'Eadhelm's Thorpe' where 'Eadhelm' was a female Anglo-Saxon name and 'Thorpe' meaning a village or outlying settlement.

The village is quite spread out, with three distinct areas – the centre around Rectory Road and Church Lane, Edingthorpe Green at The Street and The Green, and part of Bacton Road and Mill Road, which extends towards Bacton Woods. There are no longer any amenities such as a village shop or post office, but the area has a quiet rural appeal. The surrounding countryside is mainly composed of arable fields, some gently rolling, and is intersected by hedgerows, many with mature trees.

The area is crossed by many footpaths, some of which may date back to Anglo-Saxon times. This is particularly evident in lanes where the track level appears lower than the surrounding fields due to its use over many centuries. In the spring, bluebells, primroses and dog's mercury can be seen; these are also indicators of ancient paths.

The walks in this book use public footpaths and 'Quiet Lanes' and are selected to make the best of local views as well as marking interesting features along the route. 'Quiet Lanes' were established by the Norfolk Coast Partnership and Natural England to provide a network of smaller roads that link rights of way and cater for walkers, cyclists and horse riders as well as car drivers (who are encouraged to slow down, but not all understand this concept!).

Look out for the 'Quiet Lane' logo.

As well as around Edingthorpe, this book includes walks to the surrounding villages of Knapton and Paston and other areas of interest such as the Forestry Commission owned Bacton Woods, the Norfolk Wildlife Trust's Pigneys Wood and the North Walsham and Dilham Canal. Some walks use parts of the Paston Way, the local Knapton Way and the remains of the Norfolk and Suffolk Joint Railway branch line to Mundesley. Further information about what you might see is given at the start of each walk. Some walks use parts of the same routes; where this happens the details of the route are repeated to avoid too much cross-referencing.

Edingthorpe crossroads ©Gill Cullingford

The walks start either at public car parks or where one or more cars can be safely parked on a grass verge, but they can be joined at any point. Please park carefully, ensure you are not blocking any gates or field entrances and follow other guidance in the countryside code:

- Be considerate to the local community and other people enjoying the countryside
- Leave gates and property as you find them
- Follow local signs and keep to marked footpaths
- Protect the natural environment by not picking or digging up plants
- Leave no litter or other traces of your visit
- Care for nature – do not cause damage or disturbance
- Do not light fires
- Keep dogs under control and clear up after them
- Check your route and local conditions

Note that walk distances and times are approximate and the maps provide a general guide to the route only. For clarity, each map is drawn to a scale to fit the page. You are recommended to use the OS Explorer Map 252 Norfolk Coast East, which covers all the walks. Some walks can be muddy so suitable footwear is advised.

All details were accurate at the time of going to press, and we cannot be held responsible if any paths become inaccessible or if any loss or damage occurs as a result of your reliance on this book.

Enjoy your walks in this beautiful part of North Norfolk!

The Paston Way

Many of the walks use part of the 22 mile Paston Way footpath that runs between Cromer and North Walsham. The Paston Way takes its name from the Paston family who were wealthy landowners in the area. Their surname derives from the village of Paston, and they lived in an earlier house on the site of the present Paston Hall. Paston village is on the coast near Edingthorpe,

The Pastons were one of Norfolk's most prominent families from about 1380 to 1750, rising from local lords of the manor to become members of the aristocracy. They were very much involved in the politics of the Tudor and Stuart courts.

What makes the Paston family unique is that they were keen letter writers – from about 1418 to 1509 they corresponded with members of their family and others, commenting on the details of their everyday lives as well as the intrigues at court and events in the wider world. From the letters it is clear that the female members of the family played key roles in their estates and family management, which was deemed to be quite unusual at the time.

The letters, together with state papers and other documents were all preserved, and today represent the earliest and largest collection of documents in the UK detailing everyday life at that time. Most of the documents are now in the British Library.
The story of the Pastons can be explored further at:
https://www.thisispaston.co.uk/footprints01.html

Walk 1: Edingthorpe Circular

2.3 miles, 1 hour approx.

Starting at the lovely Edingthorpe Church and returning via Edingthorpe Green, enjoy the local countryside using field paths and quiet lanes. On Rectory Road you will pass thatched cottages, some dating back to the 17C, and The Old Rectory where the war poet Siegfried Sassoon spent his summer holidays as a child.

Points of Interest

The Church of All Saints, Edingthorpe
The Grade 1 listed, thatched church of All Saints dates from late Saxon or early Norman times. It has a round tower which is topped by an unusual late medieval octagonal belfry. On entering the church through the medieval south door you will see a 14C octagonal font and hanging behind it, the remains of the 12C north door, which was replaced in 2000.

Of particular note are the paintings on the north wall dating from the 14C. They show St. Christopher carrying the Christ Child on his left arm and his flowering staff in his right. Fish are swimming around his legs to indicate that he is wading through water. The Christ Child sports a halo and an orb of the world, and is giving a gesture of blessing. Further on is the remains of a tree with scenes on its branches depicting the Seven Works of Mercy, and a niche with a red and black floral surround. There may be yet more paintings under the plaster.

The rood screen, which separates the body of the church from the chancel, also dates to the 14C, and is one of the earliest surviving in Norfolk. The six panels show figures of saints, largely painted in red and green, and on top are arches with black and white spiral decorations with two tracery wheels in the centre. In the chancel is a striking modern sculpture of the Virgin Mary fronted by the Christ Child with outstretched arms. This was made by pupils at North Walsham High School.

Behind the church there is a splendid view towards Knapton, Paston and the Bacton Gas terminal. The peaceful churchyard is full of wild daffodils in spring.

Edingthorpe Church © Gill Cullingford

The lych gate is very special, being classed as a Commonwealth War Grave. It commemorates Lance Corporal Bernard John Muriel who died in the Great War. He was the son of Harvey Muriel the Rector of Edingthorpe from 1903-1922, who died in 1924 and is buried in the churchyard. His son Lance Corporal Muriel served with the 1st battalion (9th foot) Royal Norfolk Regiment from 1904, went to France in August 1914 and took part in the retreat from Mons, the battles of Le Cateau, Marne and Aisne, and the first battle of Ypres. After being invalided home, he rejoined his regiment and in April 1915 was gassed at Hill 60. On his recovery he was transferred to the 1st battalion Essex Regiment, and was drowned in August 1915 when his transport ship HMT Royal Edward was sunk by an enemy submarine on its way to Gallipoli. Others lost in WW1 are commemorated on the reverse side of the gate. A remembrance service is still held at the gate each November.

The lych gate at Edingthorpe Church © Gill Cullingford

The Old Rectory

The Old Rectory, on Rectory Road, is Grade II listed and dates from 1720, with further wings added in 1791 and 1850. Built of cut and uncut flints with brick dressings giving it a grey colour, it has a red and black glazed pantile roof. The interior has many original features.

As a child, the war poet Siegfried Sassoon spent several summer holidays at the Old Rectory with his mother and two brothers. When he revisited the village as an adult in 1937 he wrote, 'Edingthorpe, thank goodness is still a straggling hamlet'.

He described the drive from North Walsham to Edingthorpe:
'Slower and slower I drove, until I came to the signpost where four lanes meet. There was the black stagnant pond with a few ducks on it... Leaving the car at the crossroads, I strolled up the lane. The Rectory was only a couple of hundred yards away now, and I felt quite excited...'
The signpost (or perhaps a replacement!) is still there, as is the pond, and you will pass these on the walk.

Local Agriculture
The climate, landscape and soils of the local area are ideally suited for growing wheat, malting barley, oilseed rape and peas. Other important crops include potatoes and sugar beet. Some grazing of sheep and beef cattle takes place on coastal and other small areas of grassland, together with some free range pig production. Grazing land is also used for horses, and is often divided into paddocks.

Edingthorpe has a particular connection with the production of sugar beet. It was not widely grown in the UK until the early 1900s, when a Dutch company, having realised that the soil and climate were suitable, began offering growing contracts to Norfolk farmers. The beet was initially shipped to Holland for processing, but in 1912 the company bought Grange Farm at Cantley to the south east of Norwich and built a processing factory there. Representatives were sent from Holland to secure the supply by supporting local (often reluctant) farmers. They bought up and managed farms with land suitable for growing the crop. One such farm was in the neighbouring village of Paston.

In the mid-1920s, the farm manager's nephew Antonius de Feyter came to Paston for a holiday, and liking the area, asked his uncle to find him a farm to rent. Green Farm in Edingthorpe was secured; he started farming in 1929 and in 1930 married a local girl from Paston. The farm was subsequently purchased and the de Feyter family still farm there today.

In 1936 all the sugar beet factories were amalgamated to form the British Sugar Corporation, which manages the domestic crop and ensures fair pricing between growers and processors. The result is the 'Silver Spoon' sugar that we use today.

Where to park
Park at All Saints Church, Church Lane, Edingthorpe NR29 9TN.
Grid ref: TG 32277 33127
What3words: ///stars.directs.booklets

The Walk
After taking the opportunity to visit the church, start the walk by going back down the track, the way you have come, to the bottom, at the T-junction between the road on the left and the track on the right.

Turn right onto a grass track here. For part of this walk you will be following the Paston Way, which is signed by a white arrow on a pink background. There is a distant view of Knapton Church on the left. After about 200 yds, you will see a short signpost pointing left across the corner of the field, again signed Paston Way. Follow this and pass through a gap in the hedge and turn left, still following the Paston Way signs. This path has lovely open field views, with the Old School House ahead on the left. This was the village school, built in 1877 and closed in the 1960s.

There is a new barn conversion ahead on the right. This is a good place to see and hear skylarks, particularly in summer.

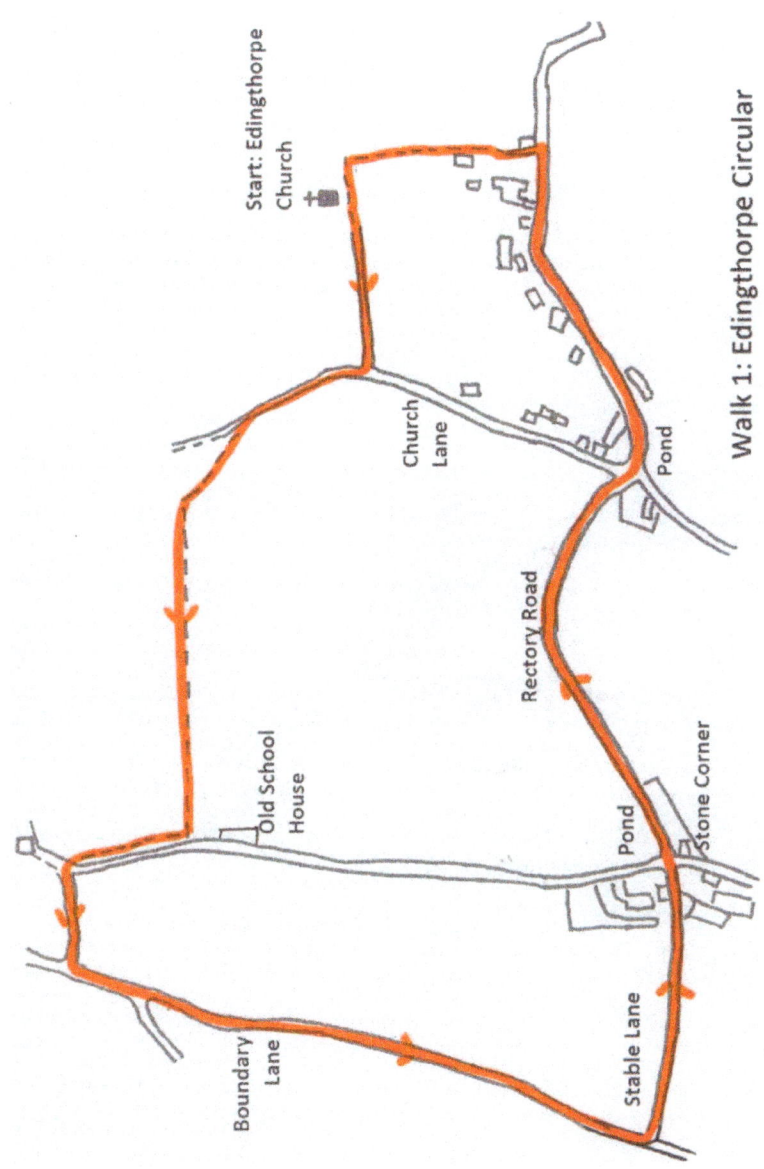

When you reach the gap in the hedge that leads to the road, remain in the field and turn right, keeping the hedge on your left, still following the Paston Way signs.

At the end of the path, turn onto the road by the converted barn and go straight on (not sharp left back the way you have come). At the T-junction ignore the right turn to Paston and Knapton, and turn left for a short distance on the road.

As the road bends round to the right, join a track that runs more or less straight ahead. This is a restricted byway called Boundary Lane and it is signed on the left after entering the track. Continue along this track, ignoring a footpath sign to the right across a field. Look out for a wide track on the left, signposted Paston Way. This is Stable Lane; take this and carry on past the stables until you reach the crossroads at The Street and Rectory Road. This is called Stone Corner, part of Edingthorpe Green.

Go straight ahead into Rectory Road, signposted Bacton, Edingthorpe via Quiet Lanes, with a pond on your left. Shortly you will see the hexagonal top of the tower of Edingthorpe Church ahead of you, framed by trees. Over the horse paddocks on the right there is a distant view of Edingthorpe Hall, an early C17 house built of flint with brick quoins, now a smart holiday let for up to ten guests.

As you come into Edingthorpe village you will reach the crossroads with Church Lane as noted in Siegfried Sassoon's memoires. On the left is the site of the village shop, last run by Myrtle Pestell, and now replaced by a modern bungalow. On your left, just in Church Lane, are a pair of listed late C17 thatched cottages, built of flint with brick dressings. The roof gable shows the characteristic 'tumbling in' of bricks set in a triangular pattern, used in buildings at this time.

Continue straight along Rectory Road with the village pond on your right. Just past the postbox on your left is The Old Rectory, which is described in the introduction above.

After 235 yards, look for the signpost set in the hedge pointing to a public footpath, signed Paston Way, Edingthorpe Church, on the left just past Church Farm Barn. This takes you through Church Farm.

Ahead of you is a modern agricultural building; take the narrow path that leads to the right of this and turn right when you reach the farm track. There is a beautiful view of Edingthorpe Church from here, also a distant view of Paston Church ahead of you, Knapton Church on the left, Bacton Church on the right, and further along, the sea. Turn left onto a narrow path in front of the churchyard, signposted Paston Way – where there is a convenient dog waste bin – walk past the lych gate and back to the car park.

http://edingthorpe-church.org.uk

Walk 2: The Three Churches

4.5 miles, 2 hours approx., plus time to spend in the churches.

This scenic walk is mostly on the Paston Way with open views towards the sea. It takes in three churches – Edingthorpe, Bacton and Paston - with a not so scenic walk by the Bacton Gas Terminal on the way, but some might find this interesting! The route is nearly all along Quiet Lanes with footpaths on the return to Edingthorpe, but there is a short stretch on the coast road at Paston. As well as the beautiful churches, you will pass the huge, thatched Paston Barn, the second largest in Norfolk.

Points of interest

The Church of All Saints, Edingthorpe – see Walk 1, page 8.

St Andrew's Church, Bacton
This flint and freestone church dates mainly to the early 15C. The porch has a niche above it with a figure of Christ and a shield above the door with 'Agincourt' painted on it. The church feels colourful and welcoming inside. The remarkable octagonal font is early C15 and has a square base with four crouching animals. The bowl has eight winged angel heads at the corners and signs of the four Evangelists and four angels with shields above. Colourful hassocks are arranged on the pews and these have carved poppy heads at the ends. The finely carved rood screen dates to the 14C. Some church restoration was carried out in 1847 and it was re-roofed in 1895.

By the entrance to the churchyard is a simple granite cross, erected as a memorial to the twelve local servicemen lost in WW1. There are a number of interesting gravestones, including the Grade II listed Montgomery memorial of 1924 which can be found outside the south chancel wall. This white Art Nouveau

stone monument has two carved angels with 1920s bobbed hairstyles and either Greek-style tunics or 1920s dress – you decide!
The church is normally open during daylight hours. Listen out for skylarks in the adjacent field.

St Margaret's Church, Paston
This is a grade 1 listed church built in the early to mid 14C on the site of an earlier church, on the pilgrim's route to Bromholm Priory. The porch was added in the late 15C. The church has two 14C paintings on the north wall; one shows the top half of a large St Christopher, and further along are parts of 'Three Living and Three Dead'. Being a reflection on mortality, this theme was popular in the years after the Black Death. The paintings show three skeletons and three rather animated noblemen, one beckoning to another.
Also of note is the organ which dates from 1889 and is grade II listed.

Paston Church in the spring ©David Beecroft

The church has many Paston family memorials. On the north side of the chancel are two huge monuments, both by Nicholas Stone, a leading sculptor and architect and master mason to James I. He was well known for his elaborate funerary memorials for prominent people of the time and was commissioned by Sir William Paston to produce a monument to his mother, Dame Katherine Paston, who died in 1628. She is shown reclining beneath a series of pillars and arches in pink and white marble, topped by a crowned skull. Her inscription is by no less than the famous poet John Donne, and tell us:

"not that she needeth monument of stone for her well-gotten fame to rest upp on, but this was reard to testifie that shee lives in their loves that yet surviving be. For untoe virtue whoe first raised her name shee left the preservation of the same, and to posterity remaine it shall when marble monuments decaye shall all".

The tomb apparently cost £340 at the time. The less elaborate classical-style monument to Sir William's father, Sir Edmund Paston, stands beside it. Beyond these are two table tombs, possibly brought to the church from Bromholm Priory after its dissolution, one thought to be for John Paston (1421-1466).

The windows contain some fine 19C and 20C stained glass and there are a number of memorials to members of the Mack family who lived in Paston Hall. Ralph Michael Mack, a Lieutenant Commander in the Royal Navy is recorded on a brass plaque as was *'lost with his ship HMS Tornado by enemy action in the North Sea December 23rd 1917'*. He had previously commanded the ship HMS Lucifer in 1914-5 and was mentioned in despatches. He is also depicted in a stained glass window by Horace Wilkinson as St Michael standing between two angels, below which are two panels showing HMS Tornado and five wild swans flying home.

Another memorial is for Arthur Paston Mack, Lieutenant Colonel of the Suffolk Regiment, who had served for some years in the Suffolk Militia and volunteered for active service again in 1914 aged 51. He was killed in September 1916 at the Somme. In WW2, Rear Admiral Philip John Mack DSO was killed in an air accident on active service in 1943.

The church is one of the locations for local author William Rivière's 1997 novel 'Echoes of War'. Apparently the Lammas family in the novel are modelled on the Mack family:

'Mrs Lammas set her wreath on the stone sill below the Archangel's feet…. On her father's arm she had walked up the aisle, treading on the tombstones, and even through her veil she had seen how radiant Michael's window had looked in the noon sun'.

Paston Barn

This enormous grade II*listed barn, attributed to Sir William Paston, was built in 1581 and is one of the largest in Norfolk, second only to Waxham barn which is 7m longer. There appears to have been some one-upmanship between the Paston and Woodhouse families following a dispute over rental income for land at Bacton, and both families embarked on competitive barn building!

The barn is built of coursed flint with brick and Lincolnshire limestone dressings with a huge thatched roof. It has two full height double doors and the roof has alternating hammer beam and tie-beam trusses, the former not really necessary for the size of the roof span, but thought to be built for bravado and show. Over the south door is a plaque inscribed:

'THE BILDING OF THIS BEARNE IS BI SIR W PASTON KNIGHTE'

Plans to turn the barn into a visitor centre were abandoned in 2002 when a colony of rare barbastelle bats was discovered in the roof, but the barn is kept in good repair and public access is permitted on specific open days.

Paston Great Barn © Adrian S Pye geography.org.uk/p/2132283

The Bacton Gas Terminal
This was built in 1968-9 and is one of the largest industrial complexes in East Anglia, covering about 180 acres. It receives and carries out some initial processing of natural gas from a number of offshore gas fields such as the Leman which is 30 miles NE of Gt Yarmouth. Supplying up to one third of the UK gas supply, it is also linked by the Interconnector pipeline to Zeebrugge in Belgium and Balgzand in the Netherlands so that gas can be exported and imported. When the gas first came on stream in 1968, it was marketed as 'High Speed Gas' by the Gas Council.

Where to park

*Park at All Saints Church, Church Lane, Edingthorpe NR29 9TN.
Grid ref: TG 32277 33127
What3words: ///stars.directs.booklets*

The Walk

Take the path that runs in front of the church and past the lych gate. If not visiting the church, carry straight on and turn right following the Paston Way sign. On passing a barn on your right, take the signed footpath on the left onto a narrow path, passing a second barn on your right. Turn left onto Rectory Road, heading in the direction of Bacton.

Ignore the public footpath sign pointing across the field on your right and carry on down the road. Just past Bacton Villas there is a distant view of the sea. Slightly further on there are also open views to the right towards the hamlet of Pollard Street and Bacton.

Just past Lark Rise on the right is a good view of Bacton Church, then after a right hand bend, there is a distant view on the right of Happisburgh Church, the red and white Happisburgh Lighthouse and Walcott Church.

On entering the village of Bacton, on the right is the Grade II listed Hall Farm Barn, a large early 18C flint barn with a thatched roof. At this stage, ignore the turning on your left signed Paston Way, St Margaret's Church and continue a short distance on the road. Take the next turning on your left with the Paston Way and a 'circular walk' signpost.
Follow the lane towards the church. A dog waste bin is provided here. After visiting the church, walk along the front to take in the sea view.

Next, retrace your steps out of the churchyard and back down the lane, turning right on the road and walking along until you are back at the thatched barn. Take the right turn you passed earlier, signposted Paston Way, St Margaret's Church Paston.

The road heads slightly downhill, with a view of the Bacton Gas Terminal ahead. There is a 'Farm Traffic' sign as the road goes round a blind bend. As you pass the Gas Terminal, note that you will be on security camera!

After nearly half a mile, you will meet the coast road from Bacton to Paston. Just before the road junction there is a view of Paston Church to the left through the trees. In spring there is a profusion of daffodils among the trees beside the road.

Turn left here, taking great care as it is a busy road with no footpath; you are heading for Paston Church on the left and will only be on this road for a very short distance.

After visiting the church head back towards the road, but take the footpath that leads to the left out of the churchyard, marked by wooden fencing and a gate. Ahead of you is the splendid Paston Great Barn (description above), open on specific days only.

Pass through the small gate at the end. Turn left onto the Quiet Lane, with woodland on either side and on the left is the privately owned Paston Hall, a two storey pale brick Georgian building.

There is a view of Knapton Church ahead on the right. Past the road junction signposted Paston, look to the left for a good view of Edingthorpe and Bacton churches. Continue along the road, now signposted Knapton. Ignore the next right hand turn signposted to Knapton and Narrow Bridge on the right and continue on the road as it bears left, now signposted Edingthorpe via Quiet Lanes.

You will shortly reach Paston Green, with the Paston Village Parish Council notice board. Ignoring a turning to the right, continue on the road, still signposted Edingthorpe via Quiet Lanes, with large mature oaks on either side.

After a third of a mile you will pass a footpath leading across a field on the right. Turn left on the road here, signposted Paston Way and Edingthorpe via Quiet Lanes. As the road bends round to the right with a barn conversion on the left, enter the field and turn right, following the Paston Way and a public footpath sign. You are now walking inside the field with the road (School Road) on your right. Look for the small marker post in the hedge opening and turn left onto the grass track between two open fields.

Along here, you can see all the three churches of your walk, Paston on the left before the trees, Bacton peeping over the brow of the hill and Edingthorpe ahead of you. The path passes to the right through a gap in the hedge and diagonally across the corner of a field. At the end you will bear right onto a track, and at the end, turn left to join the track up to the church car park.

Walk 3: Edingthorpe to the Sea

From Edingthorpe: 4 miles, 2 hours approx.
From Bacton Church: 1.5 miles, ¾ hour approx.

There are two possible starting points for this walk – from Edingthorpe along the Quiet Lane to Bacton Church and then a circular walk to the coast at Bacton, or you could park at Bacton Church and take the shorter circular walk. Either way, you will walk along scenic Quiet Lanes and across open fields towards the coast (wrap up well when a north-easterly is blowing!), visit the beach and explore part of the village of Bacton.

Points of interest
St Andrew's Church Bacton – see Walk 2, page 16.

Bacton Village
Bacton is known for its quiet sandy beaches offering miles of walking along the beach and cliffs. In 2019 the beaches were augmented by a deposit of almost two million cubic metres of sand to protect the village and the nearby gas terminal. Costing £20 million, this scheme is expected to protect the area for up to 20 years. Amenities in the village include a village shop, cafes, a fish and chip shop, Chinese restaurant and kebab house.

Bacton is also the site of the once famous Bromholm Priory, founded in 1113 as a Cluniac priory. It was once a very important pilgrimage site, as it claimed to possess a piece of the True Cross. It was dissolved in 1536. Only the ruins of the gatehouse, Chapter House and the northern transept of the Priory Church remain, and being on private land, there is no access.

Where to park
For the longer walk, park at All Saints Church, Church Lane, Edingthorpe NR29 9TN.
Grid ref: TG 32277 33127
What3words: ///stars.directs.booklets

For the shorter walk, park at Bacton Church, Church Road, Bacton, NR12 0JP.
Grid ref: TG 33524 33645
What3words: ///group.terminal.relishes

The Walk
If starting from Edingthorpe Church Car Park:
Take the path that runs in front of the church and past the lych gate. Turn right at the end, following the Paston Way sign.
On passing a barn on your right, take the signed footpath on the left onto a narrow path, passing a second barn on your right. Turn left onto Rectory Road, heading in the direction of Bacton.

Ignore the public footpath sign pointing across the field on your right and carry on down the road. Just past Bacton Villas there is a distant view of the sea. There are also open views to the right towards the hamlet of Pollard Street and Bacton.

Just past some buildings on the right is a good view of Bacton Church, then after a right hand bend, a distant view on the right of Happisburgh Church, the red and white Happisburgh Lighthouse and Walcott Church.

On entering the village of Bacton, on the right is the Grade II listed Hall Farm Barn, a large early 18C flint barn with a thatched roof. You will see Bacton Hall almost opposite on your left. A bit further on, take the turning on your left with the Paston Way and 'Circular Walk' signpost.

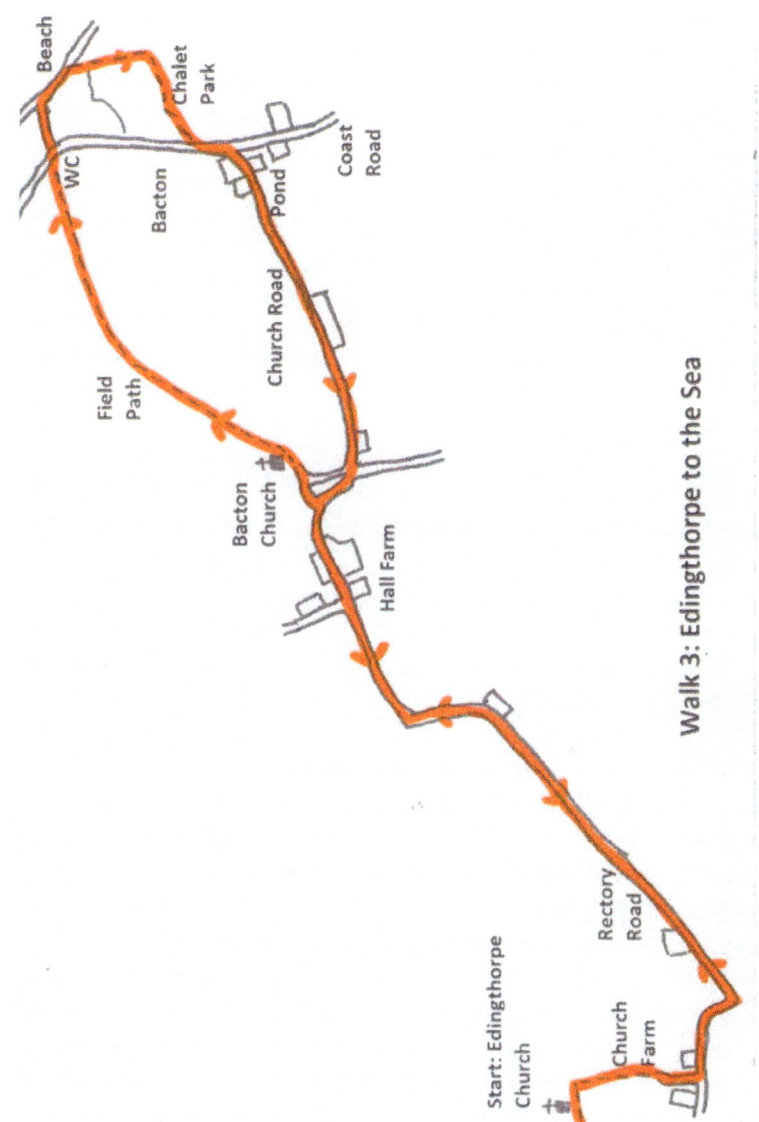

Follow the lane towards the church car park. A dog waste bin is provided here. Continue the rest of the walk below.

If starting from Bacton Church Car park:
Pass in front of the church and you will see a small metal gate ahead of you. Pass through this and follow the path across the field, signposted Paston Way. Cross a second field, still following the Paston Way sign and on a slight rise there is a seat and a view of the sea.

Pass a 'pillbox' on your right, part of the WW2 defences, as you join the outskirts of the village. Cross straight over the coast road, signposted to the Norfolk Coast path and over the second (no through road) to take the track to the beach. The house on the right facing onto the coast road is the former Ship Inn.

Turn right at the sea wall to walk along the path; if going on the beach, note that dogs are not allowed on this section between 1 May and 30 September.

Turn right along an unmade road called Mill Lane, then look out for a public footpath sign on your right (with a dog bin) which leads to a track through a private chalet park. At the end of this track you will meet the coast road, with Bacton Superstore on your left. Turn left on the coast road – there is a pavement on both sides – and cross over at a convenient point.

Take the road opposite the Bacton Fish Shop, which is Church Road and is signposted Bacton Church via Quiet Lanes. Beyond the pond on your left is a large Grade II listed barn, built of flint and brick with a thatched roof, which dates from 1762.

Stay on the road, with a Quiet Lanes sign saying Edingthorpe 1½ miles. On the right hand verge in spring and early summer is an impressive display of the umbelliferous plant Alexanders (Smyrnium olustratum). This yellow-green plant, originally from the Mediterranean and thought to be introduced by the Romans, grows very rapidly and can shade out other plants. It was originally confined to coastal regions and was cut back by cold winters, but is now thriving further inland and becoming invasive.

Look out for the sign to The Old Vicarage on the right. This Grade II listed house was built in about 1780. The front is built of knapped flint, where the stones have been split to create a flat surface and expose the shiny black or grey interior. This is expensive to produce, and is therefore used for higher status buildings, including some churches. The windows are also unusual, having scalloped hoods above them.

If you are completing the short walk:
Take the track on the right in front of The Old Vicarage sign and head for the church. Pass the church on your right and return to the car park.

If you are doing the longer walk from Edingthorpe:
Keep on the road past The Old Vicarage and head back towards Edingthorpe. After about a mile, as you approach the first houses in Edingthorpe village, look for the signpost set in the hedge pointing to a public footpath (the one you began the walk on), signed Paston Way, Edingthorpe Church. Turn right here through Church Farm.

Ahead of you is a modern barn; take the narrow path that leads to the right of the barn and turn right when you reach the farm track. Turn left onto a narrow path in front of the churchyard, signposted Paston Way, by the dog waste bin, walk past the lych gate and back to the car park.

Walk 4: A Walk Around Witton

4.9 miles, 2 hours approx.

This walk begins at Edingthorpe Church and heads south towards the parish of Witton. Using mainly field paths through attractive countryside, it follows the Norfolk Trails 'Bacton Circular Walk' for much of the route, following blue signs. It passes the interesting Grade I listed Witton Church before returning towards Bacton, with the opportunity to visit Bacton Church, then continues back to Edingthorpe along a Quiet Lane.

Points of interest
St Margaret's Church, Witton
Parts of this Grade I listed church are very early, dating to Saxon times, but the tower was built a little later and is separate to the church, with access by stairs in a turret on the west wall inside the church. The building was remodelled in the early C14 when the south aisle was added and the roof height raised to create an upper row of windows - the clerestory. The tower and the chancel were partly rebuilt in 1875 and some windows were replaced.

Inside, the font is C14 with tracery patterns on the stem and a panelled bowl. There is a mix of pews of different ages, including some fine early C18 box pews and others that were cut in Victorian times to reduce their height.

On the north wall of the chancel are two monuments – one to John Norris who died in 1734, and one to Elizabeth Norris who was married to his son, also John Norris and who died in 1769. The latter is an unusual asymmetrical structure, with a cherub on the left holding an inscription panel, held not upright, but diagonally. On the right is a display of four books whose titles are just visible, including the Bible and Shakespeare. The extraordinary whole is topped by an urn.

In 2017 the church fell victim to lead thieves; the roof has been repaired thanks to very effective fundraising by the local community. The church is usually open; otherwise the key can be obtained from the contacts provided in the porch.

St Andrews Church, Bacton – see Walk 2, page 16.

Where to park
Park at All Saints Church, Church Lane, Edingthorpe NR29 9TN.
Grid ref: TG 32277 33127
What3words: ///stars.directs.booklets

The Walk
Take the path that runs in front of the church and past the lych gate. In spring the churchyard is awash with daffodils and snowdrops. This is also a really good place to spot buzzards circling in the air around the church and adjoining fields.

Turn right at the end, following the Paston Way sign. On passing a barn on your right, take the signed footpath on the left onto a narrow path, passing a second barn on your right. Turn left onto Rectory Road, heading in the direction of Bacton. Follow the road round two sharp bends.

After approximately 350 yards, opposite two pairs of houses on your left (Bacton Villas), look out for the public footpath sign pointing across the field on your right. Take this, and you will cross the corner of the field and reach the hedge on your left where there is a yellow public footpath marker. The path leads onto the Bacton Road, where there is the first blue 'Circular Walk' sign.

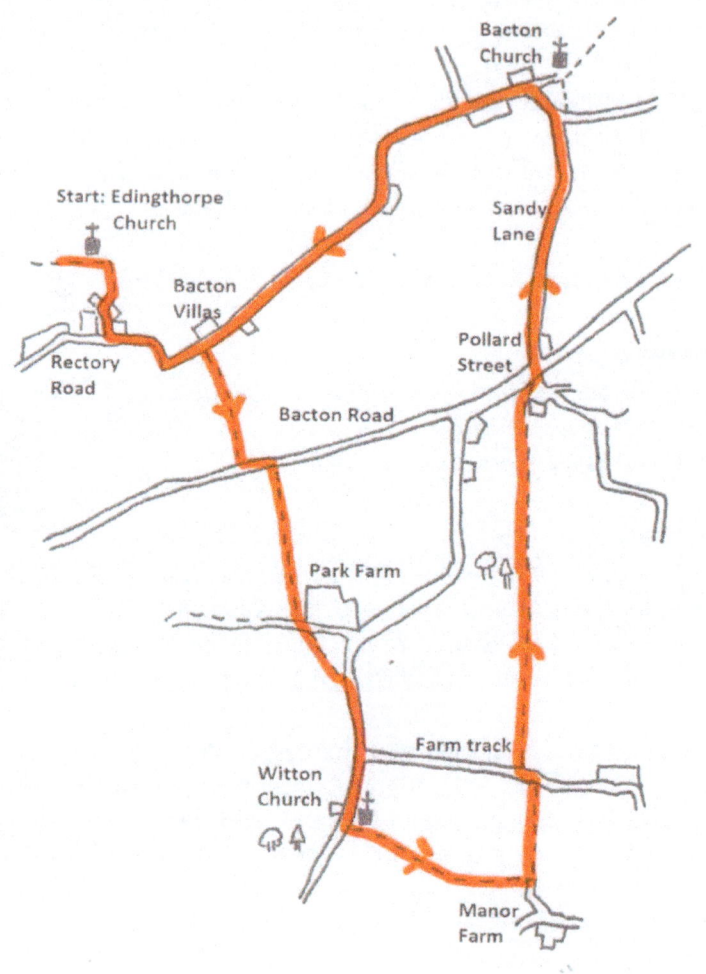

Walk 4: A Walk Around Witton

Follow the blue sign by turning left on the Bacton Road. Note that this is a very busy road with no footpath, so you are advised to carefully cross over and walk on the right hand side facing the traffic. Fortunately this section is short, and the woodland verge is accessible if you need to take refuge!

Look for the blue circular walk sign on a signpost on the left hand side of the road which is pointing right into the field, through two wooden posts and a little copse. Take this path and walk down the side of the field with the hedge on your left. There is a view of Bacton Wood (known locally as Witton Woods) on your right and views of Walcott and Happisburgh Churches and Happisburgh Lighthouse to the left, best seen through the first field gap. On the way look out for a view of Witton Hall in the distance, between the trees on the right.

You will reach Park Farm on the left, with a large modern barn. Cross over the farm track and past an old gatepost with the blue circular walk and yellow footpath markers. Go across the corner of a rough field to reach a pole with the blue walk marker. Bear left here across the field, which may not be well marked, but you are heading for two short posts straight ahead of you. On your left is Park Farmhouse with a large pond in front.

Pass between the two short posts and the hedge and turn right at the road, still following the blue signs. This will take you to Witton Church, which soon comes into view. On the right is the attractive thatched and knapped flint cottage which was formerly the village school.

Follow the path to the end of the church wall and turn left onto the car park area there, still following the blue signs, now on a public bridleway. Enter the gate in the wall to visit the church. After your visit, leave via the same gate and turn left. You are now heading for the coast, and have a view (from left to right) of Walcott and Happisburgh churches, Happisburgh lighthouse, Ridlington church and the water tower at Hill Sixty. As you go up a slight rise, there is a view of the sea towards Walcott on your left.

At the junction take the track to your left, following the blue sign. Go over the bank and into the field. Here the track may not be clearly marked, but you are heading straight ahead and after about 140 yards you will join a farm track. Turn left here and walk along the track for a short distance.

Look out for the signpost in the right hand hedgerow and turn right into a field of rough pasture – there may be livestock here, so keep dogs on a lead. You are following the right hand edge of the field and after about 250 yards will pass through another gap into a second, arable field.

Walk straight across this field, heading for the right hand corner of the wood, and walk along the track keeping the wood on your left. Further along, The Old Rectory, of pale brick and cream render, may be visible through the trees on the left, and there is a fine old barn in the distance on the right.

The path narrows to pass between two houses; this is the hamlet of Pollard Street. Turn right at the tarmac road and follow this round, passing in front of Corner Cottage, to meet the main Bacton Road.

Carefully cross the Bacton Road into Sandy Lane, still following the blue signs. The Bacton Coastguard Station is on your right. Continue along Sandy Lane, with a view of Bacton church ahead of you, plus the masts at Bacton Gas Terminal. You will reach the T-junction near Bacton Church, with a postbox on the corner.

Ahead at the junction is The Old Vicarage. This Grade II listed house was built in about 1780. The front is built of knapped flint, and the windows are unusual, having scalloped hoods above them.

To visit Bacton Church, go across the road and follow the track. To return to Edingthorpe, turn left along the road, signposted Edingthorpe via Quiet Lanes.

Continue along the Quiet Lane towards Edingthorpe for about 20 minutes. You will pass the two pairs of houses (Bacton Villas) where you turned off to cross the field earlier in the walk. As you go round the bends in the road towards Edingthorpe there is a good view of Edingthorpe Church to the right with Knapton Church in the distance to the left of it.

After passing the first two houses in the village, look for the signpost set in the hedge pointing to the public footpath, signed Paston Way, Edingthorpe Church. This takes you back, on the path you began the walk, to the church. Turn right here through Church Farm.

Ahead of you is a modern barn; take the narrow path that leads to the right of the barn and turn right when you reach the farm track. Turn left onto a narrow path in front of the churchyard, signposted Paston Way, by the dog waste bin, walk past the lych gate and back to the car park.

Walk 5: The Green to Edingthorpe Church

3.2 miles, 1¼ hours approx.

A walk along field paths and quiet lanes, with a visit to the lovely Edingthorpe Church of All Saints. The Grade 1 listed, thatched church is set on a rise amidst fields and surrounded by trees. The war poet Siegfried Sassoon visited the church when he was a child on holiday in Norfolk. It must have made an impression on him, for he later wrote in his memoires:
'It had a very special dignity and simplicity, standing there on its low hill above the harvest fields, as though it were the faithful servant of the life around it'.

Points of Interest

Edingthorpe Church, see Walk 1, page 8.

Where to park
From North Walsham, turn left off the North Walsham-Bacton Road at Edingthorpe Green and turn immediate sharp left into The Green. Drive along The Green for approximately one third of a mile. The road bends to the left past Barcham's Farmhouse (it is now known locally as Knapton Road) and about 100 yds further you can park on the left hand verge, where there is space for several cars.
Grid ref: TG 30752 32294
What3words: ///share.interrupt.foam

The Walk
If you have travelled from the North Walsham-Bacton Road, retrace your steps for about 100 yds. Ignore the public footpath sign on your right, but further on, as the road bends to the right follow the sign to the public footpath which is straight ahead (not

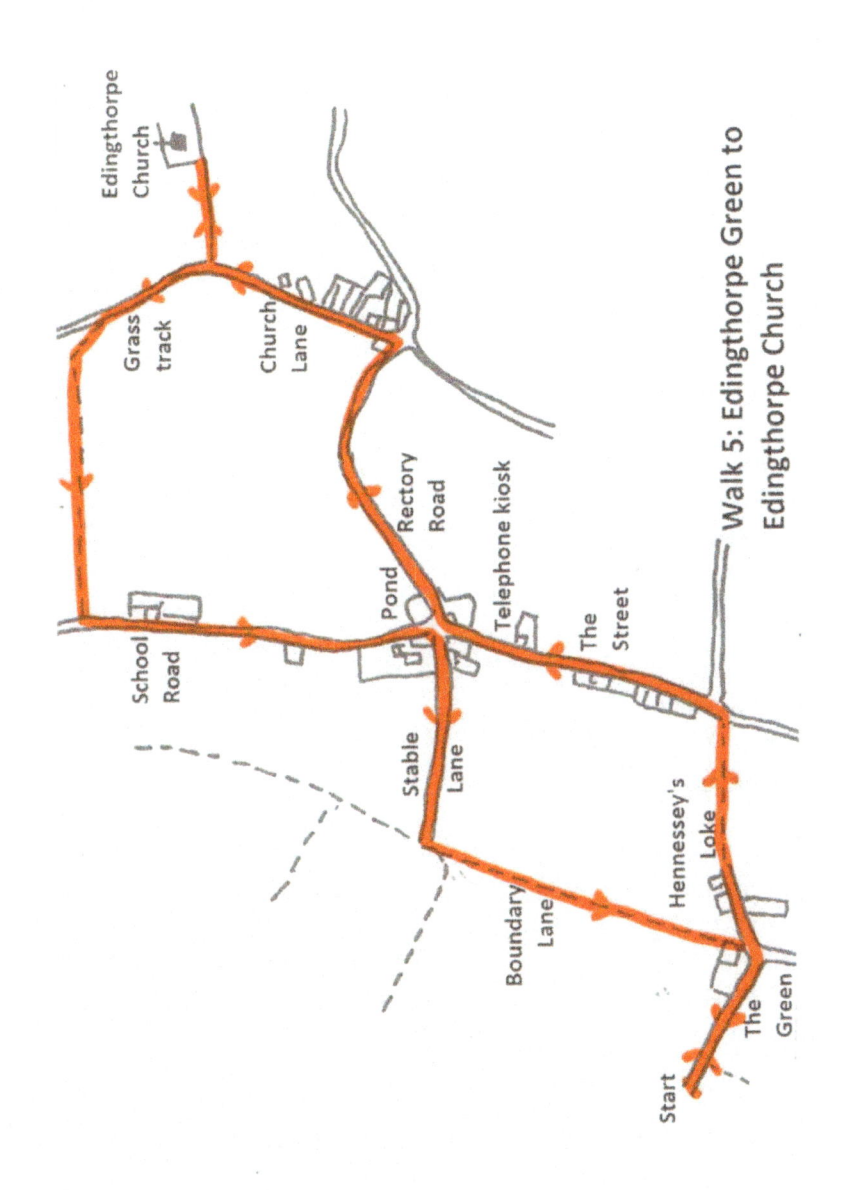

Walk 5: Edingthorpe Green to Edingthorpe Church

- Edingthorpe Church
- Grass track
- Church Lane
- Rectory Road
- Pond
- Telephone kiosk
- The Street
- School Road
- Stable Lane
- Boundary Lane
- Hennessey's Loke
- Start
- The Green

37

the one on the sharp left that is signposted 'restricted byway'). You are now entering Hennessey's Loke.

At the end of the loke (and on entering a private garden) look out for a footpath sign leading slightly to your right, through a wooded path which soon opens out with a field on your left. Pass through the metal gate at the end of the track and turn left onto The Street.

Ignore the first road to your right signposted Bacton and Edingthorpe and continue down The Street. You will pass a post box and an old telephone kiosk which is now a delightful small lending library. The house beside them was once the local shop and post office.

At Stone Corner, turn right onto Rectory Road with the pond on your left. Shortly you will see the hexagonal top of the tower of Edingthorpe Church ahead of you, framed by trees. On the right there is a distant view of Edingthorpe Hall, an early C17 house built of flint with brick quoins, now a smart holiday let for up to ten guests.

As you come into Edingthorpe village you will see a crossroads sign; the modern bungalow on your left is where the village shop once stood. Turn left here into Church Lane. Immediately on your right are a pair of late C17 thatched cottages, built of flint with brick dressings. The roof gable shows the characteristic 'tumbling in' of bricks set in a triangular pattern.

The track turns right towards the church, following the public footpath sign. Pass the car park and join the narrow track to enter the churchyard via the lych gate.

After your visit to the church retrace your steps as far as the junction with the public footpath sign and now turn right onto a grass track.

After about 200yds you will see a short signpost pointing left across the corner of the field with the white arrow on a pink background sign for the Paston Way. Follow this and pass through a gap in the hedge and turn left, still following the white/pink arrow sign. This path has lovely open field views on each side, with a distant view of Knapton Church ahead on the left (and also views of the masts at Bacton Gas Terminal).

When you reach the hedge, ignore the arrow sign pointing right, and instead turn left into School Road. The Old School on your left, constructed from cobble flint with decorative brick quoins, was built as the village school in 1877, closed in the 1960s and converted into two dwellings.

Continue along the road until you reach the pond at Stone Corner, the junction with Rectory Road, where you turned earlier. This time, turn right onto the track between some stables and a group of barns, following the white/pink sign saying Paston Way, restricted byway. This is Stable Lane.

At the end, turn left onto a wide headland path, which is a restricted byway called Boundary Lane. Boundary Lane is an ancient way, first recorded in 1797.

Ignore the restricted byway sign to the right and keep straight on as the path narrows into an old track between high banks. You will eventually reach the junction of Hennessey's Loke and The Green; turn right on The Green and after about 100yds you will reach your car.

Walk 6: Historic Transport – the Old Branch Line and the Canal

3.5 miles, 1¾ hours approx.

Starting at Edingthorpe Green, the route uses Quiet Lanes to join the old Norfolk and Suffolk Branch railway line, where you will walk both in the railway cutting and on the embankment, enjoying good views. The route returns along the North Walsham and Dilham Canal and on local field paths. With the mix of woodland and canalside, this is a good walk for watching birds and other wildlife; it is also ideal for dog walking as long periods can be spent off the lead.

Points of Interest

The Norfolk and Suffolk Joint Railway Branch Line

This line was one of the last to be built in Norfolk. The North Walsham to Mundesley section, passing through Knapton and Paston, was opened in 1898, and was extended to Cromer via Trimingham and Overstrand in 1906. The line was used to carry agricultural produce as well as passengers. Sugar beet and cereals from farms in Edingthorpe was loaded at Knapton Station.

At one time there were 17 trains a day from North Walsham to Mundesley, serving the seaside resort. It was faster to travel here from Leicester or Nottingham in 1899 than it is today! Part of the line near Cromer is still active, forming part of the Bittern Line from Sheringham to Norwich, while the section to Mundesley closed in 1953 and the other sections in 1964.

Parts of the line are used today as the Paston Way footpath, and a number of bridges and embankments survive. The line is rich in wildlife and along the old railway bed primroses (Primula vulgaris), wood avens (Geum urbanum), herb robert (Geranium robertianum) and lords-and-ladies or cuckoo pint (Arum maculatum) can be found.

The North Walsham and Dilham Canal
The canal originally ran from Antingham, north-west of North Walsham, to Wayford Bridge near Stalham, where it connects with the River Ant and hence to the Norfolk Broads. Opened in 1826, it has six locks to raise the level by 58 feet along its 8.7 mile length. The locks were sized for wherries, which were about 50 feet long.

Wherries have a distinctive large gaff-rigged sail and were able to sail along the narrow tree-lined sections of the canal, carrying up to 20 tons of cargo. They transported grain and flour to and from the various mills along the canal. Antingham had two bone mills, where bones from local butchers and slaughterhouses were crushed to provide fertiliser; manure was also transported. However, very little coal was carried as it proved cheaper to land it on the beach at Mundesley and transport overland. Tolls on canal cargo were collected near the canal entrance at Tonnage Bridge.

Use of the canal declined with the arrival of the railway and the section above Swafield locks was abandoned in 1893; this eventually reverted to farmland. The canal was last used commercially in 1934 by the wherry 'Ella'. Remaining wherries were used for tourism on the Norfolk Broads. They could be hired along with two crew members, and provided a ladies' cabin and a gentlemen's cabin, the latter also being used as a day saloon.

The North Walsham and Dilham Canal Trust (NWDCT)
As the canal was no longer in use, it was not nationalised along with the rest of the system in 1948, and therefore it is still in private ownership – one family and three companies own different sections. Over the decades the canal became choked with vegetation and many stretches dried out. The locks and bridges began to decay. In 2000 volunteers from the East Anglian Waterways Association began restoration work, and from this developed the North Walsham and Dilham Canal Trust (NWDCT) which was formed in 2008. Their regular working parties are clearing vegetation, creating new footpaths and rebuilding locks and spillways. Most notably, the two and a half mile stretch from Ebridge Mill Pond to Swafield Bridge is proving very popular for walking, canoeing, sailing, fishing, wild swimming and bird watching. At present he canal is navigable by powered boats for the first two miles up to Honing Lock.

Since clearance work began there has been a significant increase in wildlife along the canal. Visitors may spot kingfishers, grey wagtails, mute swans, little egrets, reed warblers, wood sandpipers and marsh harriers as well as deer, otters and water voles, together with some of Britain's most endangered moths and butterflies. Over 400 different plant species have been identified, including some usually found in urban areas or in sand dunes on the coast. Rare plants include the sea milkwort (Lysimachia maritima), red maids (Calandrinia ciliata), white melilot (Melilotus albus), Balkan spurge (Euphorbia oblongata) and bifid hemp nettle (Galeopsis bifida).

Where to park

From North Walsham, turn left off the North Walsham-Bacton Road at Edingthorpe Green and turn immediate sharp left into The Green. Drive along The Green for approximately one third of a mile. The road bends to the left past Barcham's Farmhouse (it is now known locally as Knapton Road) and about 100 yds further you can park on the left hand verge, where there is space for several cars.

The Walk

Continue on foot out in the same direction and you will soon come to a crossroads marked by a give way sign. This is called 'Dead Man's Grave' on local maps, and probably indicates the burial place of a so-called 'self-murderer'. Committing suicide used to be viewed as both a sin and a crime, the corpse being quietly buried somewhere in the countryside at night, usually near a crossroads. Such graves remained unmarked.

Walk straight on over the crossroads, signposted 'Trunch and Knapton via Quiet Lanes'. You will come to two footpath signs, a restricted byway on your right and a footpath on your left. Ignore these for now, but the walk will return on the left hand footpath. Carry straight on, and at the next, slightly staggered, junction also go straight ahead into the lane signed 'Unsuitable for HGVs'.

Pass over the old railway bridge and look out for a small, unsigned path on the left where the wooden fence ends. This leads to some steps that lead into the railway cutting. At the bottom is a sign board for Knapton Cutting and the Butterfly Nature reserve. The Butterfly Nature Reserve is visited in Walk 8 (or you could make a short detour by turning left to the end of the cutting and back).

Walk 6: The Old Branch Line and the Canal

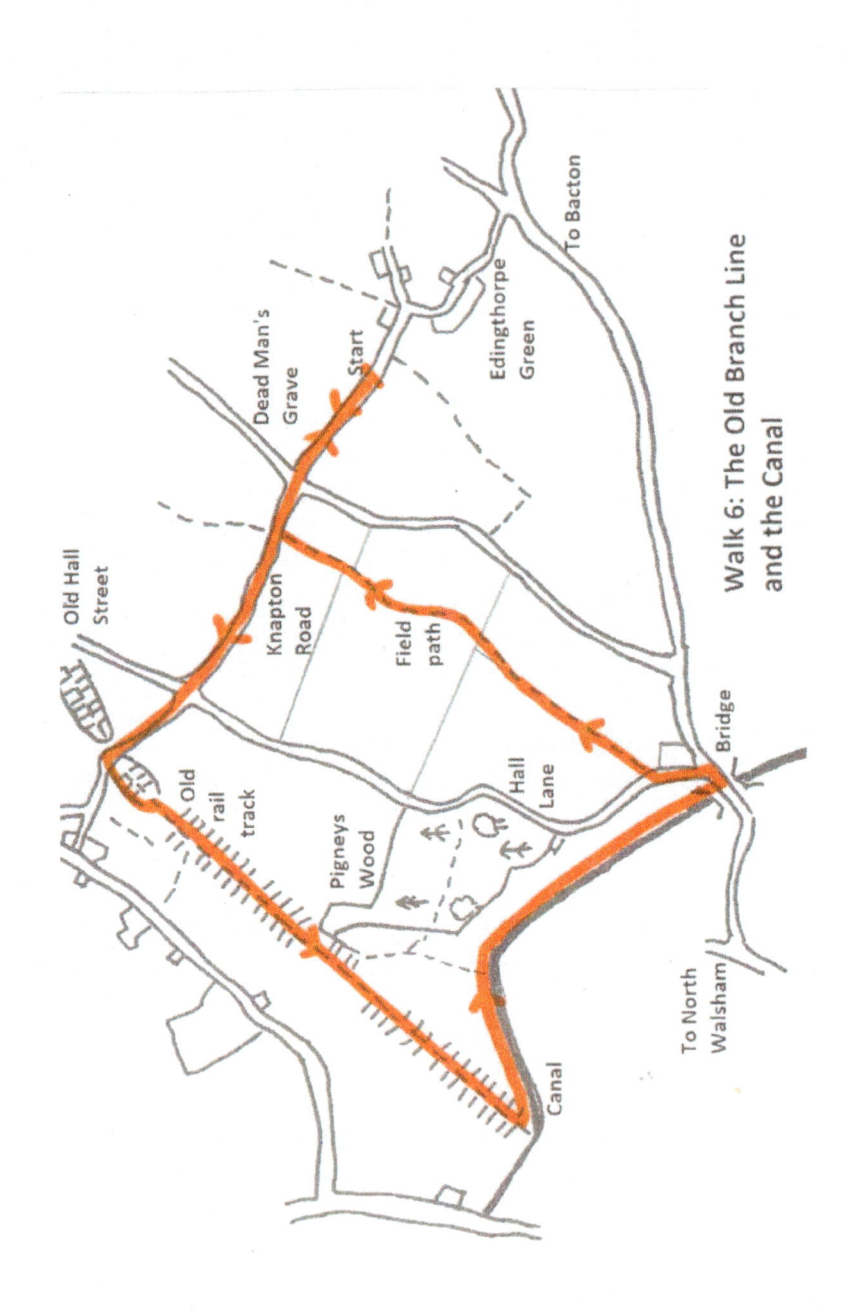

Turn right at the bottom of the steps. You are now on the track of the old Norfolk and Suffolk Joint Branch Line. As the ground falls away, the line follows an embankment with views to the right.

Cross over the wooden bridge, and you will have reached the edge of Pigneys Wood on your left, the subject of a separate walk (Walk 9).

A second bridge passes over a farm track, and eventually the path comes to an end with a blocked off footbridge. Take the left hand path that leads towards the canal (signposted Paston Way) and then turn left to walk along the canal bank. This section is a permissive path (where the landowner has granted access).

About half way along is an entrance sign to Pigneys Wood, but continue along the (now public) footpath along the canal bank.

Just after the spillway you will reach a parking/works area and the North Walsham-Bacton Road. Turn left to join the road very briefly; it is probably safest to remain on the left hand verge, but do take care on this busy road.

Take the left turn into Hall Lane.

After a short distance look out for the house sign 'Rivermount' on the right, and turn right here by the metal gates and follow the 'Public Footpath' sign into the field, where you will be walking on a headland path with the hedge on your right. Attractive views open up on the left.

The path (signed public footpath) passes through a gap in the hedge to the right and cuts across the corner of the field. On leaving the field, take the path straight ahead of you which is signposted 'public footpath' (but only back in the direction you have come!) Take this anyway, and you will be on a grass path between two fields.

Go through the gap in the bank and then cross the arable field, which has usually been marked out, but otherwise head for the signpost in the distance.

On reaching the lane (opposite the concrete standing area) turn right, back to the crossroads at Dead Man's Grave and straight across into The Green, which is also signposted to North Walsham and Edingthorpe via Quiet Lanes.

Continue along The Green for a short distance and you will reach your car on the right.

Bacton Wood Mill Lock ©David Beecroft

Walk 7:   The Green to the Knapton Angels.

3.2 miles, 1¼ hours approx.

A walk along ancient walkways and field paths, particularly good for dogs as there are long stretches where they can be off the lead. The highlight is a visit to the Grade I listed St Peter and St Paul's Church, Knapton.

Points of Interest

St Peter and St Paul's Church, Knapton
This stunning church, in the centre of Knapton village, dates from the 14th century but was restored in 1882 by Sir George Gilbert Scott. It is constructed of flint with ashlar dressings.
The magnificent interior has a soaring late medieval double hammer beam roof with a total of 160 ornately carved and painted flying angels carrying scrolls, shields or musical instruments. It is said to be one of the finest in Norfolk. The 13C Purbeck marble font has a beautiful white octagonal font cover from 1704. Interestingly, this is inscribed, in Greek, 'NIYON ANOMHMA MH MONAN OYIN ' and is a palindrome (that reads the same backwards as forwards). Translated this reads 'wash my sins not my face only', a wonderful inscription for a font! In the chancel is a late 16C combined reading desk and chair with carved bench ends. There are also some ancient coffin lids, some with carved decorations, which pre-date the church. The church tower is topped by a striking cockerel weather vane said to have been designed by the Norwich School painter John Sell Cotman (1782-1842) who once lived nearby.

Where to park
From North Walsham, turn left off the North Walsham-Bacton Road at Edingthorpe Green and turn immediate sharp left into The Green. Drive along The Green for approximately one third of a mile. The road bends to the left past Barcham's Farmhouse (it is now known locally as Knapton Road) and about 100 yds further you can park on the left hand verge, where there is space for several cars.
Grid ref: TG 30752 32294
What3words: ///share.interrupt.foam

The Walk
Continue on foot out in the same direction and you will soon come to a crossroads marked by a give way sign. This is called 'Dead Man's Grave' on local maps.

Continue straight on over the crossroads, signposted 'Trunch and Knapton via Quiet Lanes' until you come to a concrete hard standing. Just past this on the right is the path, which is signposted 'Restricted Byway'. This is Green Lane, an attractive path which bends between high banks with mature oak trees and elderly hawthorns on either side. There are carpets of celandines, daffodils and bluebells in the spring and a number of gently decaying old oak stumps.

Look out for a curious little shrine on your left with a cross marked 'Pearl and Freddy', perhaps someone's much loved pets. Further along on the left is a huge heap of freshly dug soil, possibly a badger sett. Before long you will see, through the trees on the left, the outskirts of Knapton village and the church tower.

Walk 7: The Green to the Knapton Angels

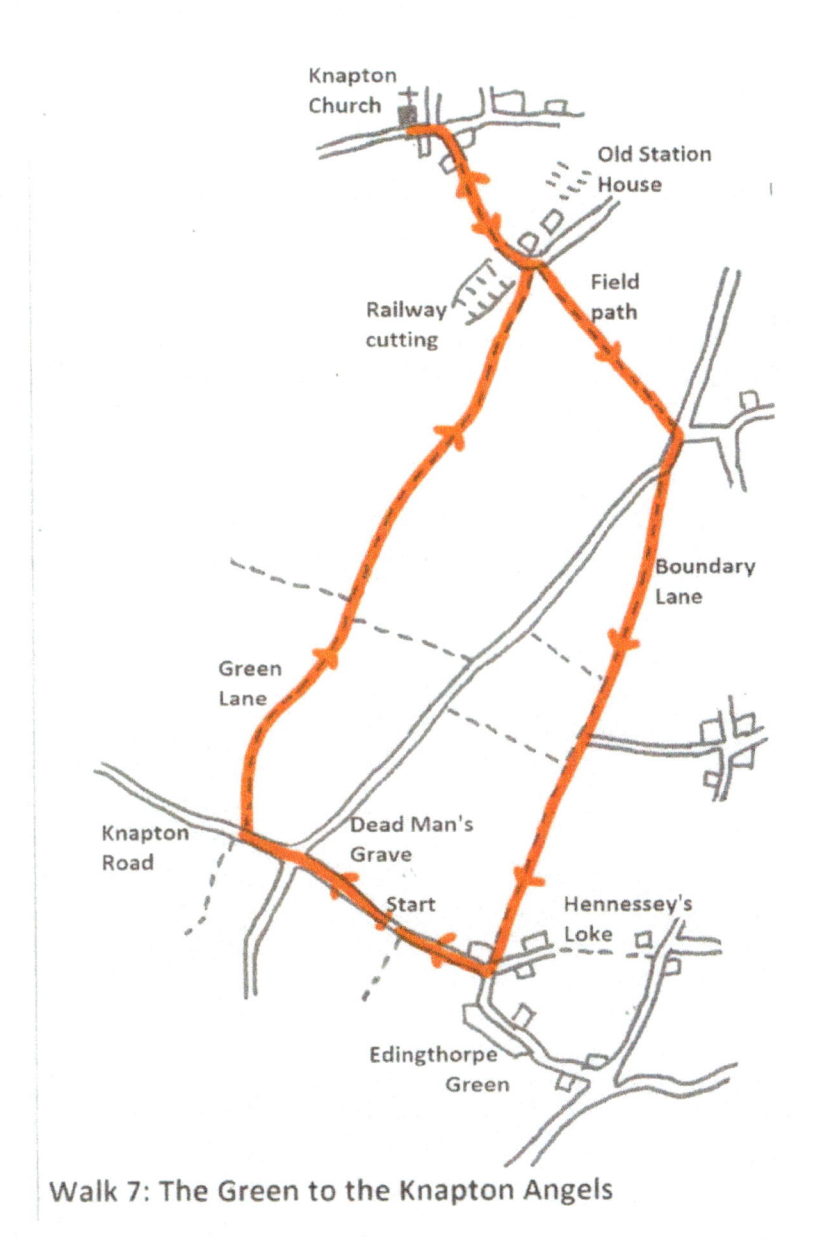

Ignore the sign off to the right to the Paston Way, and a bit later, the sign to the left, and continue straight along the restricted byway. Look out to the right for the square tower of Bacton Church and a glimpse of the sea. Further along you will have a view of the hexagonal-topped round tower of Edingthorpe Church on your right. Just before the end of the path there is a very good view of Knapton Church (where you are heading) to the left.

At the end of the path is an information board entitled 'Explore the Paston Way' with a map. Turn left here along a narrow track, signposted Paston Way (white arrow on pink background) and St Peter and St Paul's Church Knapton. Keep to the boundary of the house on your right, which was originally the old station house for Knapton Station, now much developed.

Go over the old railway cutting that once carried the Norfolk and Suffolk Joint Railway branch line to Mundesley. If you look over the bridge, part of the old station platform is still visible. This line opened in 1898 and closed in 1964.

You will be on a narrow footpath leading directly to Knapton which passes through a bank and turns right across a field, still following the Paston Way sign. The track becomes a gravelled lane called Timber Loke; turn left when you reach the road, signposted 'St Peter and St Paul's Church', which is clearly visible. Enter the churchyard through the lantern arch and enjoy the splendours of the church. It is usually open from dawn to dusk.

After visiting the church, turn left and retrace your steps, turning right into Timber Loke and back along the track.

When you reach the 'Explore the Paston Way' map sign again, keep the sign on your right and enter the footpath that goes diagonally across the field which is signposted 'Paston Way, Edingthorpe Church 1 Mile'. Although an arable field, it is usually marked out, although muddy when wet.

Pass to a second field through a gap in the hedge still following the Paston Way sign. Join the road through a wide gap and turn right, again following the Paston Way sign and passing the red and white marker for the route of the Bacton Gas pipeline.

Ignore the road on the left signposted 'Edingthorpe via Quiet Lanes' and continue for a short distance up the road. As the road bends round to the right, join a track that runs more or less straight ahead. This is a restricted byway called Boundary Lane and it is signed on the left after entering the track.

Continue for about three quarters of a mile along this track, ignoring restricted byway signs to the left and right and keeping straight on as the path narrows into an old track between high banks. This is an excellent place for seeing butterflies in the summer, particularly meadow brown, orange tip and ringlets.

You will eventually reach the junction of Hennessey's Loke and The Green; turn right on The Green and after about 100yds you will reach your car on the left.

For further exploration of the Knapton area, Knapton Parish Council have published a selection of walks on their website: https://knaptonvillage.org/our-village/walks/

Walk 8: The Butterfly Walk

2.7 miles, 1¼ hour approx. (longer walk)
0.9 mile, ½ hour approx. (short walk)

Noel Coward's famous observation 'flat, Norfolk' made in his drama 'Private Lives' does not apply to this walk! Using a number of field paths, you can enjoy the pretty rolling countryside between Knapton and Swafield. You will walk along the section of the old Norfolk and Suffolk Joint Railway Branch Line cutting known as the Butterfly Walk, and return along Quiet Lanes with open views.

There is an option to take a short walk from the car park at Knapton cutting, along the Butterfly Walk and returning via attractive field paths.

Points of Interest

The Norfolk and Suffolk Joint Railway Branch Line – see Walk 6, page 40.

The Butterfly Walk
The section of the old railway used in this walk is called the Knapton Cutting Butterfly Reserve. It is a designated local nature and butterfly reserve, where 19 different species of butterfly have been recorded, including the red admiral, small tortoiseshell, small skipper, small copper, common blue, meadow brown, peacock, gatekeeper and ringlet.

The cutting is a mixture of neutral and acid grassland and sandy embankments which support a range of different wild flowers on which the butterflies thrive. Plant species include black knapweed (Centaurea nigra), yarrow (Achillea millefolium), sheep's sorrel (Rumex acetosella), primrose (Primula vulgaris), oxeye daisy (Leucanthemum vulgare) and hoary or silver-leaved cinquefoil (Potentilla argentea).

Also found, and of particular note, is the rare small-flowered catchfly (Silene gallica), which is classified as critically endangered in the United Kingdom. This looks like a smaller flowered white campion, but with sticky stems and leaves. It is an annual, best seen in June or July, growing on the sandy embankments.

Where to park (longer walk)
From North Walsham, turn left off the North Walsham-Bacton Road at Edingthorpe Green and turn immediate sharp left into The Green. Drive along The Green for approximately one third of a mile. The road bends to the left past Barcham's Farmhouse (now known locally as Knapton Road) and about 100 yds further you can park on the left hand verge, where there is space for several cars.

Where to park (short walk)
Travelling from Edingthorpe, follow the directions for parking for the longer walk, but drive straight on, over the first crossroads, and turn right at the second crossroads onto Hall Lane. Park in the small public car park, which is signed on the left, in Old Hall Street.
Grid ref: TG 30081 33068
What3words: ///defectors.dips.prance

The Walk
Longer Walk
Continue on foot out in the same direction, listening out for the distinctive 'little bit of bread and no cheese' call of yellowhammers, and you will soon come to a crossroads marked

Walk 8: The Butterfly Walk

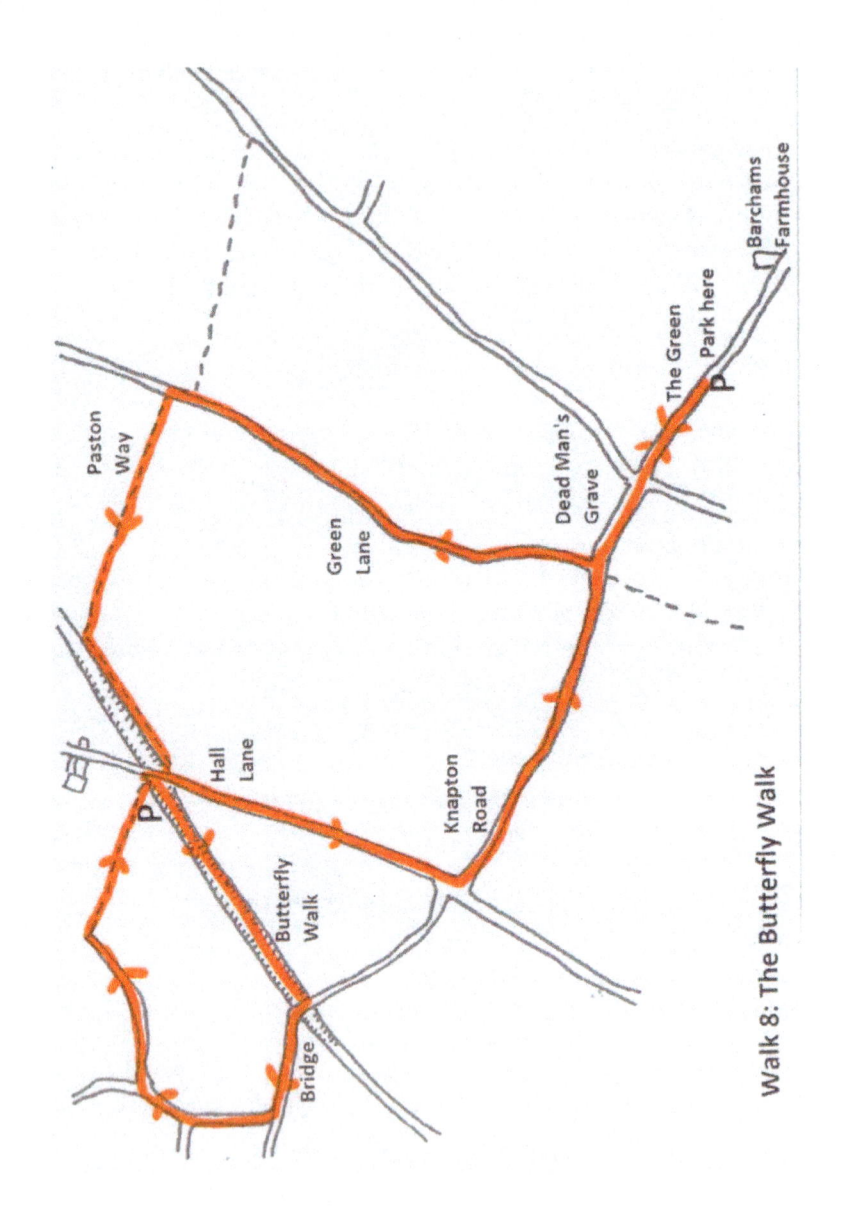

by a give way sign. This is called 'Dead Man's Grave' on local maps, and probably indicates the burial place of a so-called 'self-murderer'. Committing suicide used to be viewed as both a sin and a crime, the corpse being quietly buried somewhere in the countryside at night, usually near a crossroads. Such graves remained unmarked.

Continue straight on over the crossroads, signposted 'Trunch and Knapton via Quiet Lanes' until you come to a concrete hard standing a short distance up the road. Just past this on the right is the path, which is signposted 'Restricted Byway'. This is Green Lane, an attractive path which bends between high banks with mature oak trees and elderly hawthorns on either side. There are carpets of celandines, daffodils and bluebells in the spring and a number of gently decaying old oak stumps.

Further along on the left is a huge heap of freshly dug soil, possibly a badger sett. Before long you will see, through the trees on the left, the outskirts of Knapton village and the church tower.

After some distance, ignore the sign off to the right to the Paston Way, but approximately 50 yards further on look out for a second sign, sited on the right but pointing to the left, also signed Paston Way and public footpath. Turn left here, through a gap in the hedge.

The path climbs up to cross an open field, arable but usually marked out; you are heading for the edge of a trimmed ornamental hedge. Skylarks can be heard here from early spring. Pass through a low bank into a second field, and cut across the corner of this, heading for a gap between the hedge and a wire fence.

Turn left here along a narrow path between the hedge and wire fence, and you will soon reach Hall Lane. Cross straight over into a small car park. There is a red and white gas pipeline marker and a signpost to Pigneys Wood and North Walsham. There is a dog waste bin here.

The short walk starts here:
Take the steps down into the railway cutting and enjoy the Butterfly Walk. This part of the cutting is just over a quarter of a mile long, and quite deep but relatively open, thus suitable for the wild flowers that support the butterflies. There is an occasional seat.

The bridge indicates the end of this section, and there is a signboard with information about the Butterfly Walk (and pictures of the butterflies you might have seen). Take the steps on the right just after this board and join the road at the top, turning left and heading downhill. This is a pretty piece of undulating countryside with good views, including Trunch Church.

Follow the road as it bends to the right; it then bends to the left with a thin metal gate ahead of you. Take the footpath that goes straight ahead here, a restricted byway. Through the trees to your left is a view of the cream-rendered late 16C Swafield Hall, which is grade II listed and set in beautiful formal gardens.

At the fork in the path, take the path on the right, with a blue public bridleway sign, which may not be visible until you pass a bush in the centre of the fork. You are now walking on a field boundary with mature trees on your right and this should be followed for a quarter of a mile.

Ignore a wide field entry on the right. A little further on, the path bends to the right through a gap and you will be walking on another field edge, with the hedgerow on your left.

Turn right when you reach the road, Hall Lane, and arrive at the car park. The short walk ends here.

To continue the longer walk:
Leave the car park and turn right along Hall Lane. Please note that although designated a Quiet Lane, this road can be quite busy with traffic. It is best to walk on the left hand side here, as there are more opportunities to step off the road and let vehicles pass.

After a quarter of a mile you will reach a road junction; turn left here onto Knapton Road (usually much quieter) and walk along here passing the entrance to Green Lane where you turned off earlier.

On reaching the crossroads at Dead Man's Grave, go straight across onto The Green, and you will reach your car on the right.

The small flowered catchfly

(Silene gallica)

Walk 9: A Walk Around Pigneys Wood

3.5 miles, 1.5 hours approx. (Longer walk)
1 mile, 40 mins approx. (Shorter walk)

Starting at Edingthorpe Green, take field paths and Quiet Lanes towards Pigneys Wood to enjoy this wildlife reserve. The diverse range of habitats, from woodland, wetland and heathland support a rich community of mammals, birds, butterflies and dragonflies. Return on Quiet Lanes. For a shorter walk, drive to the car park at Pigneys Wood and walk around the wood from there.

Points of Interest

Pigneys Wood
The wood covers 23.5 hectares (58 acres) of land about 2 miles northeast of North Walsham. Originally grazing land with two small wooded areas, it was purchased by the North Norfolk Community Woodland Trust in 1993 and converted to mixed woodland. Over 20,000 trees of 40 different species were planted. Wetland areas near the canal were also restored to increase the range of habitats and there is an area of heathland on the upper slopes. The Norfolk Wildlife Trust took over in 2017, and are continuing the conservation management work by enhancing the range of habitats present as well as making the site more accessible for visitors to enjoy.

As you walk through the wood you will notice areas where young trees such as hazel have been coppiced. Coppicing is a traditional method of woodland management in which young tree stems are periodically cut down near ground level and the new growth, consisting of long straight stems, is used for traditional woodland products such as fencing, stakes and pea sticks. Management in this way creates a continuous supply of timber, but also benefits wildlife.

By the late 1800s harvesting timber from coppices was no longer financially viable and the woodlands were left to grow a dense canopy of taller trees, shading out plants which grow on the woodland floor, resulting in the loss of many wildlife habitats. The coppicing practised here will enable the ground layer plants such as bluebells and wood anemone to thrive again.

In this wildlife-rich reserve, birds such as the goldcrest, nuthatch, Cetti's warbler and red kites have been spotted, as well as the red admiral, peacock and holly blue butterflies. Nearer the canal, dragonflies such as the emperor, migrant hawker, black tailed skimmer and Norfolk hawker have been recorded. Otters, water voles and badgers are also present. The rare Camberwell beauty butterfly was recorded in November 2011 and a bittern in March 2013.

There is an impressive 450-year-old ancient oak tree called 'the Old Oak' which is next to a small woodland area with a carpet of bluebells in spring. Two walks are signposted from the car park; our walk uses parts of these.

Where to park
For the longer walk:
From North Walsham, turn left off the North Walsham-Bacton Road at Edingthorpe Green and turn immediate sharp left into The Green. Drive along The Green for approximately one third of a mile. The road bends to the left past Barcham's Farmhouse (it is now known locally as Knapton Road) and about 100 yds further you can park on the left hand verge, where there is space for several cars.

For the shorter walk:
Park at the Pigneys Wood car park on Hall Lane. From Edingthorpe, take the Bacton Road towards North Walsham. Just after the road sign indicating a junction on a left hand bend, turn right into Hall Lane, which has a brown 'tree' sign, and after about ½ mile turn left into the Pigneys Wood car park.
Grid ref: TG 29657 32245
What3words: ///screamed.readjust.foster

The Walk
Longer walk
Continue on foot out in the same direction and you will soon come to a crossroads marked by a give way sign. This is called 'Dead Man's Grave' on local maps, and probably indicates the burial place of a so-called 'self-murderer'. Committing suicide used to be viewed as both a sin and a crime, the corpse being quietly buried somewhere in the countryside at night, usually near a crossroads. Such graves remained unmarked.

Continue straight on over the crossroads, signposted 'Trunch and Knapton via Quiet Lanes' until you come to a concrete hard standing. Just past this on the left is the path, which is signposted public footpath. Go up the bank and across the arable field, usually marked out, and heading for the electricity pole and between two bushes.

Go over the bank into a second field, this time walking along the right hand edge. Cross over the field track into another field, signposted public footpath, with the path cutting across the corner of the field. You are heading for another electric pole and the ruined tower of North Walsham church.

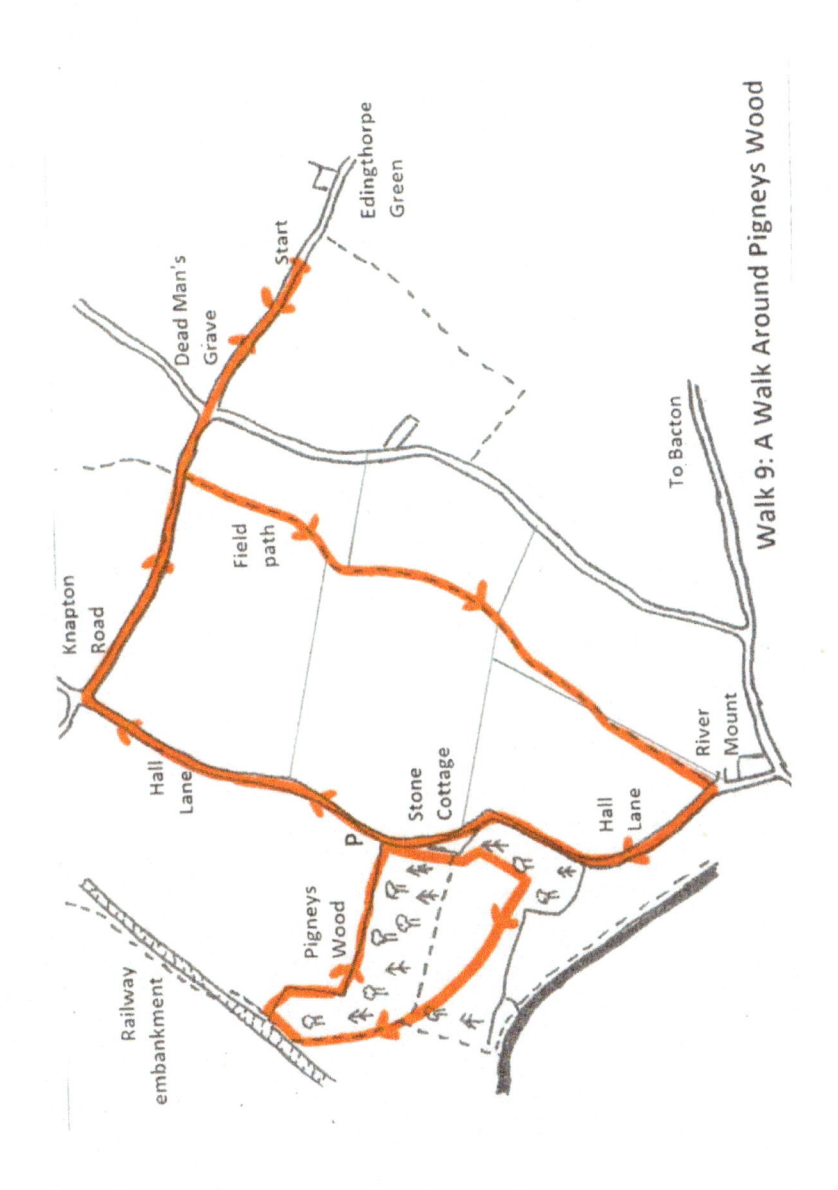

Walk 9: A Walk Around Pigneys Wood

At the end of the field turn left onto a wider track, still signposted public footpath. You are now walking down the side of the field with the hedge on your left.

Go through the metal gate at the bottom of the track and turn right onto Hall Lane. The road sweeps round to run alongside Pigneys Wood, and just past Stone Cottage you will see the sign to the Pigneys Wood car park on the left.

The shorter walk begins here.
From the car park, pass through the metal gate. There is a Norfolk Wildlife information board about the wood on the left. Continue on this track; when it goes off to the right (with two large green storage containers visible) carry straight on.

The path takes you through mature birch trees with some undergrowth, mainly brambles, then opens into a glade with another path on your right. Continue straight on here.

Turn right on the next path, just before the canal water meadows, following the red arrow. This is quite a wide track through alder, willow and hazel, passing through an open area, and eventually reaching an old barn on your left.

Go straight ahead on the path past the barn which is signposted public footpath (ignoring the path to the left). Keep straight on the main path which goes slightly uphill. Ignore the path to the right which goes steeply up the hill and continue on the main path towards a big wild cherry tree, with a post with a red arrow just past it.

As the path narrows you will see an area on the right where hazel is being coppiced, in order to open up the canopy and encourage wildlife. The railway embankment comes into view on your left.

Avoid the stairs leading to the top, but follow the path along the base of the embankment, walking through a sunken area with a high bank on the right as well. This is an ancient trackway and is marked by a yellow arrow.

On reaching the red and white gas pipeline sign, head to the right up two steps and keep on the left hand fork. This narrow path leads uphill and takes you on a loop around some heathland, dominated by gorse, with good views at the top.

Follow the yellow arrow pointing right through the heathland and back down into a wooded area. At the junction of the two paths turn left, up two steps and eventually you will pass through a grove of conifers.

After passing a large holly bush you will reach an area of open fields; turn left here, and perhaps take the opportunity to rest on the seats provided whilst enjoying the open views. The barn you passed earlier is at the bottom of the hill.

When ready, continue on, keeping the seats on your left and following the red and yellow arrows. Avoid the path to the right and you will arrive back at the car park (and a convenient dog waste bin).

To continue the longer walk, turn left onto the road. Turn right at the first crossroads and you will eventually reach the entrance to the footpath where you set off across the fields earlier.

Continue straight on, over the crossroads at Dead Man's Grave and straight across into The Green, which is also signposted to North Walsham and Edingthorpe via Quiet Lanes. Continue along The Green for a short distance and you will reach your car on the right.

Walk 10: Royston Bridge to Ebridge Mill

3.5 miles, 1.5 hours approx.

A walk along the raised banks of the North Walsham and Dilham Canal with views over fields and marshland, to Ebridge Mill, returning through Bacton Woods.

Points of Interest

The North Walsham and Dilham Canal – see Walk 6, page 41.

Ebridge Mill
There are records of a mill at Ebridge as far back as 1537, but the existing mill was owned by Cubitt and Walker from 1869 and produced flour until 1966. Most of the original machinery was then dismantled and, now powered by electricity, was used to produce animal feed. The waterwheel was removed in 1972. The mill was sold to Duffields in 1998 and subsequently closed. It has now been converted into six homes which retain many of the original features.

Bacton Wood - see Walk 12, page 74.

Bacton Wood Mill
The earliest record of Bacton Wood Mill was in the Domesday Book. The present building dates from 1747, and was modified in 1825 in anticipation of the canal opening and the expected increase in trade. The cast iron waterwheel was 18 feet in diameter and 8 feet wide, providing enough power to turn three sets of stones. As a young man, Sir William Cubitt (1785-1861), worked here with his father, Joseph. In 1807 he invented self-regulating windmill sails, first installed at Horning and Stalham. He later became a famous civil engineer, involved in building,

railway and waterway works. He was knighted in 1851. The mill was last used commercially in 1944, by which time it was powered by diesel. It was converted into living accommodation in 1967.

Where to park
Park on a rough area of land at Royston Bridge on the North Walsham - Bacton Road. If coming from Edingthorpe/Bacton it is on the right just before the bridge. Be aware this area can be quite muddy, and may occasionally be closed during the ongoing canal work.
Grid Ref: TG 29742 31415
What3Words: ///music headlines rewriting

The Walk
Carefully cross the road and join the track by the NWDCT information board. This is a permissive path (i.e. not a public right of way) where the landowner has granted access along the path. Therefore please keep dogs on a lead at this point. The track is raised along the canal bank, giving good views over Purdy's Marsh on your left and surrounding fields.

After 350 yards, take the turn to your right on a wide bank across the canal, then turn left so that you are walking on the opposite bank, now on a public footpath. You will shortly arrive at Bacton Wood Mill Lock which is being restored by NWDCT volunteers; the top gates have been fitted, complete with metal balance beams salvaged from the old gates. An information board provides further details. The canal is watered beyond this point.

The path continues between the canal and some workshops (once used as a silo for the mill, and now headquarters for the NWDCT) and you will see a narrow, humpbacked bridge ahead, which is grade II listed. Join the road, Anchor Road, Spa Common

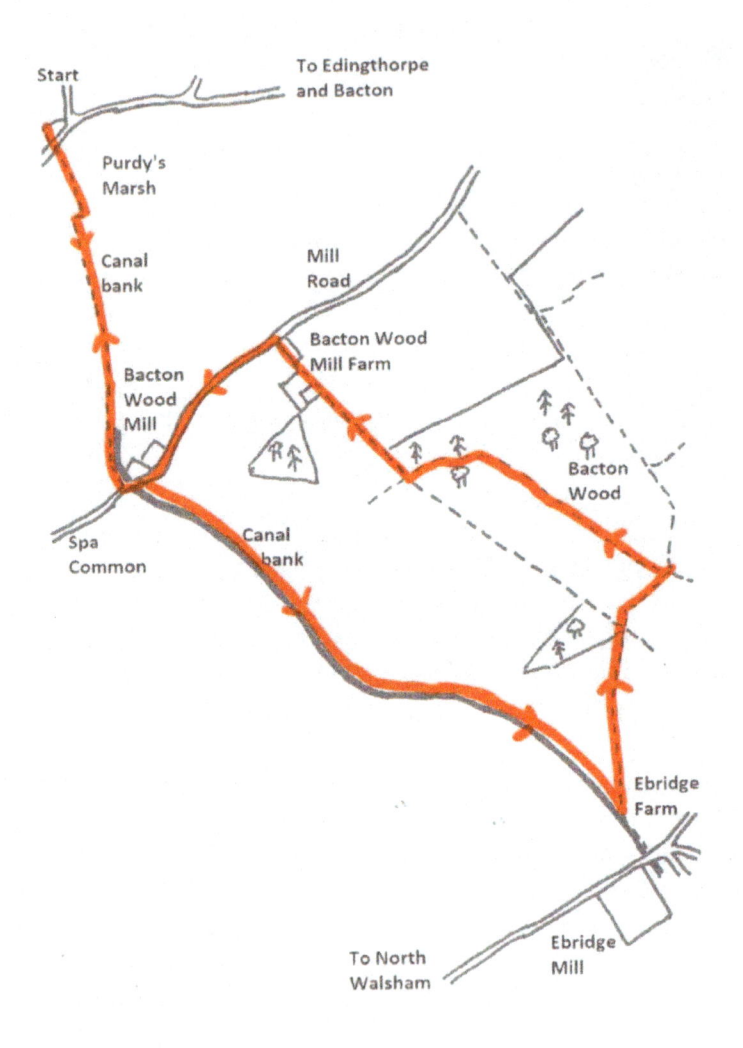

Walk 10: Royston Bridge to Ebridge Mill

and turn left over the bridge, passing a post box on your right.

After a second small bridge turn right in front of a WW1 'pillbox', a concrete guard post built in 1916 in response to the threat of a German invasion on the East Coast. This formed part of a second line of defence which ran along the course of the River Ant, and has a rare, semi-circular shape. Another NWDCT information board is placed here.

You are now on a second permissive path, along the raised bank of the canal, with lovely views. As you walk, you will be able to see the five-storey Ebridge Mill ahead, and Bacton Woods on a rise to the left. At Ebridge the canal widens and is a popular area for water sports, including wild swimming! The NWDCT offer trips in their solar-powered boat Ella II from here.

Walk for about ¾ mile, and ahead of you is a spillway, which takes excess water from the canal to prevent flooding. Turn left (and slightly back on yourself) here, through a metal gate and onto a public footpath through Ebridge Farm. Turn right through the gate at the end, still following the yellow public footpath sign.

Turn left onto a wide track with open fields on your right and a high hedge on the left, which then crosses an open field before joining Bacton Wood. You may see buzzards circling above the trees here.

On entering the wood, follow the blue public bridleway sign, bearing right at a slight T-junction and then left onto a wider track with a blue and red marker. In this area, you can see bluebells in spring. This is open access Forestry Commission land and there are many criss-crossing paths, but attempt to stay on the main path. This is a lovely walk between mature silver birch trees and the occasional conifer. The paths can get quite muddy underfoot after wet weather.

You will reach a triangle of land with a seat; turn sharp left here just before the triangle, following a blue marker. Some heathland opens up on the left, which has recently been planted with young trees and fenced off. Keep left at the end of the fencing.

Continue through the wood, then bear left at the next T-junction (a post with two small green dots is opposite) where the path heads downwards and through a hedge to the field boundary. A perimeter footpath joins from the left, and ahead of you is a sign saying 'Private, no public right of way'. This is the start of the return track – if you have missed it by taking a different path through the wood, attempt to head for the wood's left (or south-west boundary) where you should pick up the boundary path.

Turn right on the track and shortly you will come to the entrance to Bacton Wood Mill Farm. The track is bordered by bluebells, greater stitchwort and other wild flowers in late spring. Please stay on the track and pass through the metal gates, heading towards the road. This is Mill Lane, a Quiet Lane, where you turn left.

As the road descends, the ochre coloured Bacton Wood Mill is visible on your right, and you will be back at the 'pillbox' where you turned along the canal before.

Retrace your steps by again taking the path on the right just after the bridge, pass the workshops on your left and the lock on your right. Return along the canal bank, remembering to turn right over the canal again (the path appears to carry on but leads to a dead end), cross the North Walsham-Bacton Road and return to your car.

Walk 11: Around Little London

2.5 miles, 1 hour approx.

A walk along the North Walsham and Dilham Canal, starting at Royston Bridge and taking a circular route through the marshes and local lanes of the area called Little London. The name possibly comes from the Anglo Saxon word 'Utlenden' used to describe strangers or foreigners, which when written down in the Middle Ages would have become Litillondon. Visit the end of the canal at Swafield Bridge and return via a short detour into Pigneys Wood.

Points of Interest

The North Walsham and Dilham Canal – see Walk 6, page 43.

Pigneys Wood – see Walk 9, page 58.

Where to park
Park on a rough area of land at Royston Bridge on the North Walsham - Bacton Road. If coming from Edingthorpe/Bacton it is on the right just before the bridge. Be aware this area can be quite muddy, and may occasionally be closed during the ongoing canal work.
Grid Ref: TG 29742 31415
What3Words: ///music headlines rewriting

The Walk
Royston Bridge is where the Bacton Road passes over the canal, and here the canal has been culverted. This was done when heavy vehicles needed to reach Bacton Gas Terminal, but now the works traffic uses another route and it is hoped that in the future the bridge may be reinstated.

Walk 11: Around Little London

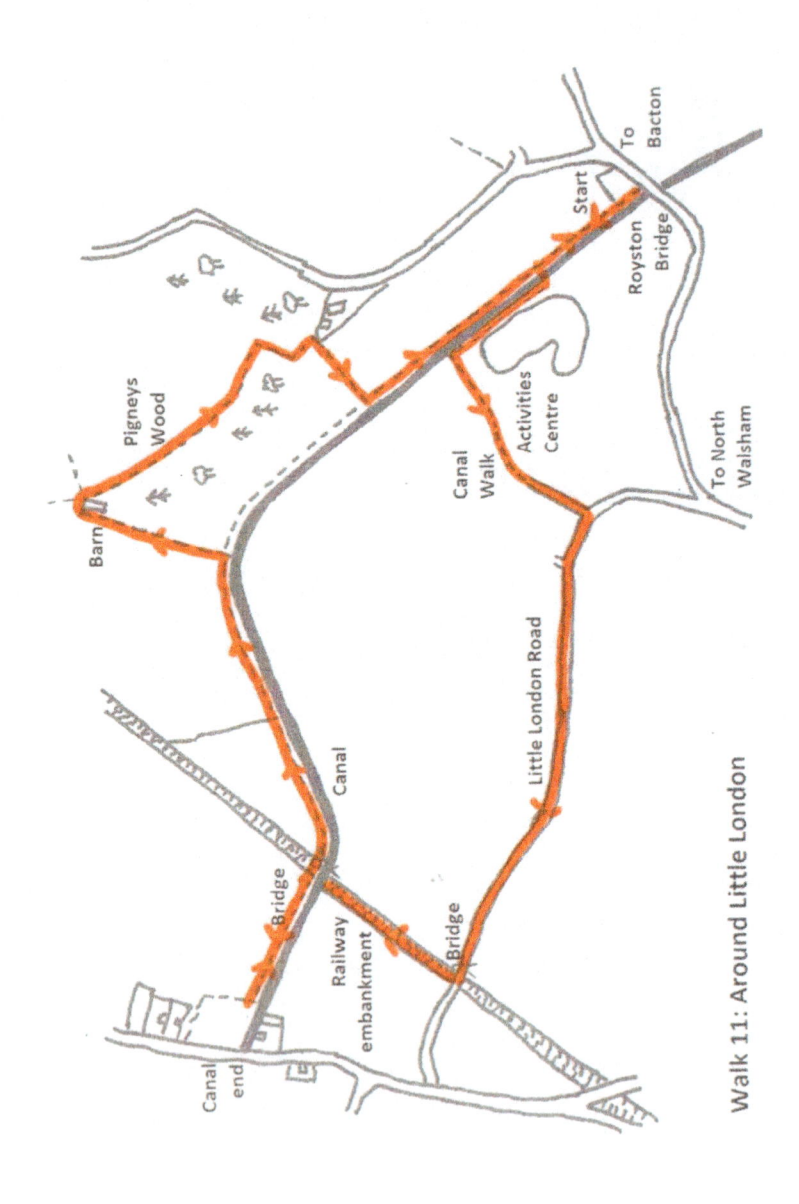

Begin by heading away from the Bacton Road along the canal. You will be walking between the canal on your left and the spillway on the right. By the sluice gate, where the canal is filled in, forming a land bridge, cross over to the opposite bank. The local water treatment plant is visible on the right across the canal.

Go over the wooden bridge on your left, signposted Canal Walk, permissive path. Follow the track through some rough pasture. The Mike Thurston Water Activities Centre, where young people camp and learn water skills, is on the left. Look out for the resident heron! Join the track that leads from the centre, going straight on.

On reaching Little London Road, turn right, still signposted Canal Walk. This is a pretty rural road with mature trees on both sides. Ignore the Canal Walk sign further along on the left (which heads into North Walsham) and continue along the road. The railway embankment is visible on your right.

After approximately half a mile you will reach the remains of the old bridge over the road, where the arch has been removed. Take the steps on the right just past the bridge that lead onto the railway embankment, signposted Paston Way. This is a deeply wooded section, with several tree species including birch, hazel, sycamore, holly and mature oaks.

At the end, the way is barred to protect a gas pipe that crosses the canal on a bowstring bridge. Take the steps down on the right and at the bottom turn left to cross the canal by the wooden footbridge.

Turn left off the bridge, walking with the canal on your left. This is a short detour to view the end of the canal at Swafield Bridge, which is the limit of public access along the canal. It was also the turning point for the wherries when the section above Swafield locks was abandoned in 1893; scrape marks on the bridge point to the difficulty of turning in such a small area! The long, low building over the canal was once a coal store. A pair of kingfishers are regularly seen here.

This is the end of this section of the walk, but you might want to consider turning right and walking out onto the road to visit Tavern Tasty Meats, a butcher specialising in meat from traditional Norfolk breeds, including some award winning sausages! Otherwise, retrace your steps back along the canal, which should now be on your right. On the left is a field of blackcurrants, belonging to Swafield Fruit Farm, suppliers to Ribena.

Pass under the railway bridge, this time going straight on. After a quarter of a mile you will reach a sign board for Pigneys Wood, and our route turns left here, taking about 15 minutes (0.4 mile) through part of the wood; alternatively you could continue straight along the bank of the canal until you reach your car.

If taking the wood detour you will walk through a marshy area (where the path can be very boggy in wet weather) and then into the wood. Turn right past the old stone barn (which has shelter and some seats). Then, ignoring the main path that goes straight ahead, turn immediately right onto the path that crosses the field, then entering a wide path through trees, which include alder, hazel and willow.

Look out for a brass plaque to the left in the trees, which details the planting of the sessile oaks (Quercus petraea) in this area. This type of oak was used for shipbuilding in the 19th century, and they were planted here in 2005 to mark the 200th anniversary of the Battle of Trafalgar.

At the end of the path, turn right again, following a yellow arrow, back through water meadows towards the canal.

Turn left when you reach the Pigneys Wood sign at the canal bank and continue straight on, pass the spillway, and back to your car.

Walk 9 describes a longer walk in Pigneys Wood. Alternatively there are other marked paths you can follow in the wood to create your own walk.

Footbridge over the Canal © Gill Cullingford

Walk 12: Bacton Wood Circular

1.3 miles, ¾ hour approx.

The entire area of this lovely wood is open access, with many paths and it is quite easy to get lost! This walk is intended to be an introduction to the wood, using the 'red' marked route, which follows wide, well-made tracks which are easy to follow. It should be buggy and wheelchair friendly, unless it has been very wet. The route passes the pond, the 'grandparent' oak tree and Gibbet Piece (although the exact position of the latter is not clear). A (not buggy friendly) detour is suggested to the ancient pot boiling site. Alternatively you could choose to follow one of the other colour-marked trails. There are picnic tables and a waste bin near the car park, plus an information board with a map showing the main routes. A map can also be downloaded from https://www.north-norfolk.gov.uk/media/2109/bacton-wood-leaflet.pdf

Points of Interest

Bacton Wood
Bacton Wood, also known locally as Witton Woods, covers over 280 acres and is owned by the Forestry Commission. The northern area was once ancient broadleaved woodland and the central and southern area were heathland, unsuitable for agriculture because of the sloping land and poor soil. The ancient woodland area has been managed to enable natural regeneration, and plants such as bluebells, wood sorrel and dog's mercury grow underneath. New planting from 1956-1971 has resulted in areas of mixed woodland, open heathland with heather, broom and gorse, and plantations of conifers such as Scots and Corsican Pine, Douglas Fir, Western Hemlock and Larch.

There are about 30 species of tree in the wood, some native and some introduced, but all are managed sustainably. There are two sessile oaks thought to be over 200 years old. The whole provides for a rich diversity of animals, birds and insects.

In the south of the wood is a Bronze-age burial mound; there is also a pond and an ancient pot-boiling site, where stones were heated to boil water. An area near the north western end is marked 'Gibbet Piece' and in 1797 had a sinister tale attached to it. Will Suffolk, a father of four, had been having an affair with a local girl, Mary Beck. When her brother discovered what was happening, he ordered them to end the affair. They met on 5 February and an argument followed, during which Will beat Mary to death with a stick. Will was taken into custody and hanged at Norwich Castle on 17 March before being 'gibbetted' – hung on a gallows in the wood to be exposed to public ridicule. The body was displayed for six years before being taken down and buried in an unmarked grave nearby. A small mound of earth beside one of the tracks, now overgrown with scrub, is thought to mark the spot. It is said that the sound of the gibbet's creaking can sometimes be heard on the breeze!

Where to park
The Forestry Commission Bacton Woods Car Park at Wood Cottages, Old Hall Road. Nearest postcode NR28 9UE.
Grid ref: TG 31706 31192
What3words: ///troubled.lifestyle.bothered

The Walk
Cars are parked in small bays within the wood. The best way to find the start of the walk is to head back onto the access road that you used to enter the wood and pass round the closed barrier (with black and yellow bands) which will be on your right. This leads into a wide track with shallow ditches on both sides;

Walk 12: Bacton Wood Circular

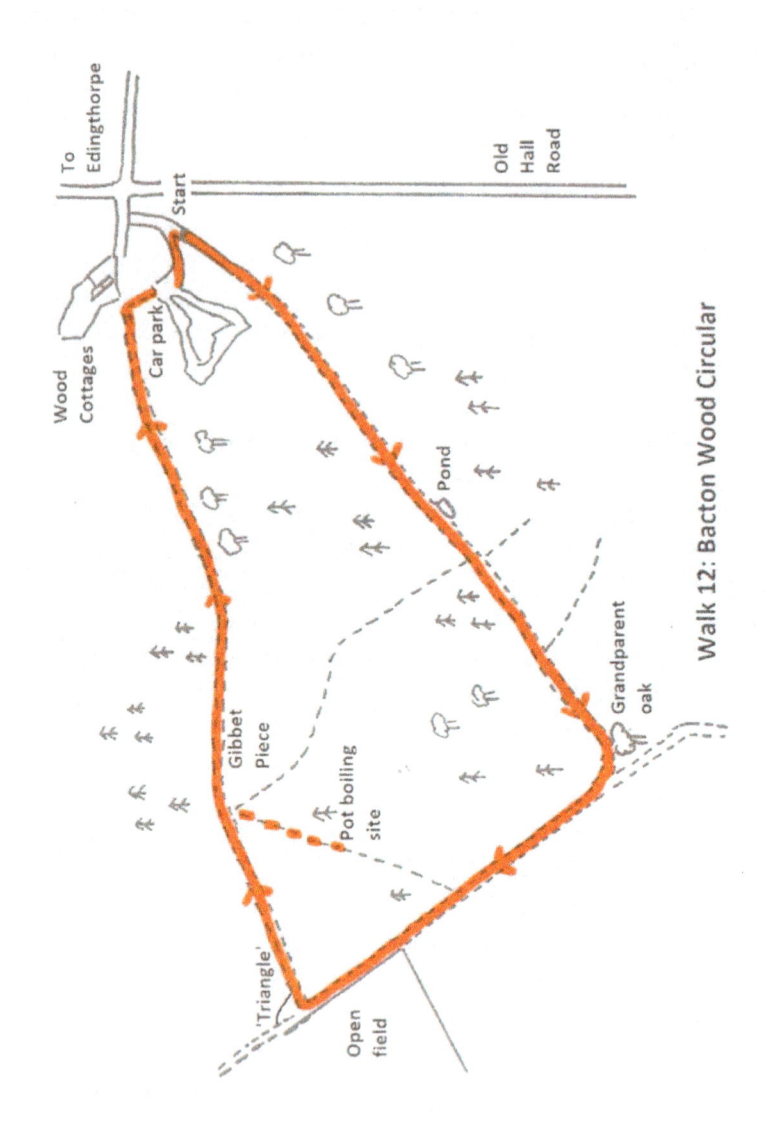

- To Edingthorpe
- Old Hall Road
- Start
- Wood Cottages
- Car park
- Pond
- Grandparent oak
- Gibbet Piece
- Pot boiling site
- 'Triangle'
- Open field

76

after passing a wide crossroads (with one path on the right leading back to the car park), you should see a red and yellow marker ahead of you; go straight on. The land rises on the left hand side with fine views through the trees and a bit later on there is an impressive stand of pines on the right.

After a few minutes you will reach the pond on your left, then later, another red and yellow marker, and a seat on the right, rather hidden in the bank. The route opens up into a small clearing and several paths come in from the left, but continue straight on.

After a further few minutes, the sessile or Cornish oak (Quercus petraea) with its split into four trunks, comes into view on the left. This is thought to be over 200 years old. The path veers slightly to the right at this point and later, there is a yellow marker on the right, followed by another seat.

The path goes gradually uphill and a field opens up on the left. There is a blue and yellow marker at this point. Carry straight on until you reach a small triangle of grass where a smaller path goes straight on while the main one veers right. Keep right on the main path, which has now become a public footpath.

Keep straight ahead, ignoring a further, wide path going off to the left. The tree growth is thinner here, mainly silver birch and sweet chestnut. There is another red and yellow marker on the left. Slightly further on the left is an area of forest that has been recently cleared.

At the start of the cleared area, you will come to a place where two paths go off to the right. This is opposite a post with a green 'Quiet Lanes' and yellow footpath signs, found on the left. If you would like to take a detour to the ancient pot boiling site, take the first path (that goes slightly back the way you have come). Although unmarked, the site is possibly in a hollow on the right, where there is also a water source. It is reported that shards of flint may be found here, the remains of the stones that were heated and then placed either under or inside the pots to boil water.

After visiting the pot boiling site, retrace your steps back to the junction and turn right to re-join the main path. It is in this area that the Gibbet Piece once existed, but the exact spot is unclear. On the edge of the cleared area on the left, a row of beech trees frame the view of the countryside beyond.

The path becomes very wide, rather like an avenue, with beech trees on either side. There is a blue and yellow marker on the right and a seat on the left. As the path narrows again towards a barrier, turn right to return to your car.

Bacton Wood in the spring   ©David Beecroft

Acknowledgements

I would like to thank Margaret and Graham de Feyter for providing much of the interesting local history.

Richard and Vanda Barker, David and Gillian Beecroft and Caroline Cousins generously spent time walking the routes and checking my directions and the distances involved.

David and Gillian also provided additional information on the natural history of the area.

I am very grateful for their help; any remaining errors are mine alone. Any updates or corrections can be emailed to gillcullingford@gmail.com.

Printed in Great Britain
by Amazon